History of the

Israeli Sherman-based Self-Propelled Weapons

Volume 1

Tom Gannon

Trackpad Publishing

"God fights on the side with the best artillery."
(Napoleon Bonaparte)

"Without support, the infantry won't move!"
(IDF Artillery Corps motto)

Language

Due to the author's American origin, American spelling has been used in this book.

Photographs

Some of the photographs in this volume are not of the best quality. There is a scarcity of in-service photos to be found through normal archival sources and personal contributions. Due to their rarity and historical value, and their importance in telling the full story, it was felt important to include them.

Cover captions

Front Cover: The quintessential example of Israeli Sherman-based artillery is the *TOMAT* M50 155mm self-propelled howitzer, described in detail in Chapters 3 and 4. This vehicle has just passed the reviewing stand during the 1964 Independence Day parade, in the southern city of Be'er Sheva. (Fritz Cohen, Israeli Government Press Office)

Back Cover 1: The main entrance to *Beit Ha'Totchan* features what is said to be the former home of a member of one of the town's founding families. The displays include prototypes, test subjects and weapons and vehicles retired from service. The L33 *Ro'em,* in the foreground, is described in detail in Chapter 7. To the left, in the photo, is a test vehicle from the shared US Army/IDF HIP (**H**owitzer **I**mprovement **P**rogram) program, which ultimately led to the development of the M109A6 Paladin, while the last vehicle is one of the *Merkava*-based 155mm *Sho'lef* self-propelled howitzers. Neither of these last two vehicles saw active Artillery Corps service.

Back Cover 2: The exhibits at *Beit Ha'Totchan* are placed along dirt paths that wind through the trees, making for a very tranquil setting. The buildings in the background are in the town itself.

Back Cover 3: The Hatzerim Air Base is located in the Negev Desert near Be'er Sheva. Public access is restricted to the museum only. The *Kilshon* shown here is described in detail in Chapter 9.

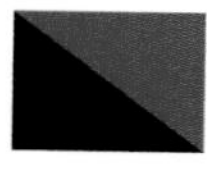

Israeli Artillery Corps Insignia

Israeli Defence Forces Flag

Contents

The Author

Born in January, 1949, the author grew up near Baltimore, Maryland in the United States of America. A business credit manager by profession, his hobby interests include armor modeling and researching Sherman tanks and the Israeli Defense Forces. He is a regular visitor to various Internet armor discussion forums, and has presented seminars on armor subjects at model shows in the US.

He is married to the love of his life, Connie Baker. Between them, they have four children and five grandchildren:
Bryan Gannon
Heather (Gannon) Eyler, married to Herb, with granddaughter, Julia
Melissa Baker, with granddaughters, Cora and
Charlie Ann
Justin Baker, married to Laurie, with grandsons, Dylan and Reid

Previous works include:
Israeli Sherman, Tracing the History of the Sherman Tank in Israeli Service, 2001
Israeli Half-tracks, Volumes One and Two, 2008
Israeli Sherman, Second Edition, 2017

This photo was taken at *Yad La'Shiryon*, during the 2005 Memorial Day week celebrations and commemorations.
From left to right: Alex von Reizen and Jan-Willem de Boer (Netherlands), Joshua Weingarten (USA), David 'Didi' Levy (Israel), me, Michael Mass (Israel, Curator at the Latrun museum)

Introduction

Gunpowder-based artillery dates back as far as the early 1100s, in the Far East. It became a factor in Europe during the Hundred Years War (1337 to 1453), and it continued to be so during and beyond the campaigns of Napoleon. As a former artillery officer himself, Napoleon made extensive use of massed batteries, firing on a concentrated set of targets. Toward the end of the American Civil War (1861 to 1865), rifled cannon became dominant, essentially destroying the effectiveness of masonry or stone fortifications. As the concept of indirect fire took hold later in the 19th Century and throughout World War I (1914 to 1918), artillery lived up to its nickname of 'King of Battle'. World War II (1939 to 1945) saw its prominence continue, in both the use of standard tube weapons, as well as in the effective use of rockets.

This work discusses the contribution of, primarily, self-propelled artillery in the development of *TZAHAL* (*Tzva Ha'Hagana Le Yisrael* or the Israel Defense Force or IDF) as it was paired with another significant part of IDF history, the American Sherman tank.

This subject is best understood by also discussing what came immediately before the Sherman-based artillery weapons in IDF service. Actually, the use of weapons more powerful than rifles and machine guns in the region pre-dates the establishment of *TZAHAL* (*Tsva Ha'Haganah le'Yisra'el,* Hebrew for Israel Defense Force or IDF), which did not occur until May 26, 1948, nearly two weeks after independence.

The tensions between Jews and Arabs further pre-dates what became known as Mandatory Palestine. To protect the various *kibbutzim* (collective agricultural settlements) and *moshavim* (cooperative settlements) in the *Yishuv* (the Hebrew word used to define the region), Jews paid Arab guards and a Jewish organization, *Bar Giura.* In 1909, a new group called *Ha'Shomer* (The Watchmen) absorbed the latter and, following the 1920 Passover Riots, the Jews established what almost immediately became a clandestine force, *Haganah* (The Defense).

More openly, during the so-called Arab Revolt in 1936, the British realized that they needed help to keep the peace or to at least control the extent of the violence. Therefore, they authorized the Jews to create an organization called the *Notrut,* whose members were commonly referred to as *Notrim* or Guards (singular form is *noter).* Composed of the Jewish Supernumerary Police (*Shotrim Musafim,* restricted to the actual settlements) and the more mobile *Manin* (*Mishmarot Nayim,* or Mobile Guards), which quickly evolved into the highly-mobile Jewish Settlement Police (*Misteret Ha'Yishuvim Ha'Iviryim*) in 1937, they added much needed strength to settlement protection.

The joint British/Jewish strike force, known as the Special Night Squads (*Plugot Ha'Layla Ha'Meyukhadot*) joined the *Notrut* in 1938, at the suggestion of British Captain Orde Wingate, and during World War II, *Haganah* openly organized *PALMACH* (acronym for *Plugot Mahatz,* 'Strike Forces') in 1941, laying the groundwork for the later IDF. All of these forces used weapons supplied by the British, along with others obtained by acquisition teams around the world. Everything from small arms, mortars, armored and non-armored vehicles and, eventually, artillery were in the mix.

Towed guns and howitzers, along with a variety of mortars, were the most common types of artillery during the formative years of what became the IDF's Artillery Corps (*Heil Ha'Totchanim*) from the mid-1940s through to the early 1950s. Weapons used, prior to and during the War of Independence (1947 to 1949), varied from homemade mortars such as a small number of the locally-designed and built *Davidka* (Little David), to the obsolete pre-World War I *Napoleonchik* howitzer, and the very effective ex-British QF (Quick Firing) 25-pounder gun/howitzer. Small quantities of other vintage or near-vintage pieces, dating back to both World Wars, were also acquired from various sources, and used to a limited degree.

IDF artillery is prominently featured at several locations in Israel:

Beit Ha'Totchan (Gunners' House) is a memorial and museum dedicated to the fallen members of *Heil Ha'Totchanim* (IDF Artillery Corps). It is located in the picturesque northern town of Zichron Ya'akov, close to the coast. The main building is surrounded by acres of trees and paths, along which one can see exhibits depicting many of the towed and self-propelled artillery pieces used over the years. In a plaza in front of the main building, are stone pillars bearing the names of 756 fallen artillerymen.

Batey Haosef (IDF Collection Houses) is in old Yafo (Jaffa), now part of Tel Aviv. Its displays include a number of artillery pieces, mortars and historical vehicles. It is here that one can see most of the older towed guns.

Yad La'Shiryon (IDF Armored Corps Memorial and Museum) is located 9.2 miles (15 kilometers) west of Jerusalem, on a hilltop near the historical town of Latrun in the Ayalon Valley, next to the main highway from Tel Aviv. It is often simply referred to as 'Latrun'. The town itself dates back to the time of the Crusades. Ancient Christian strongholds bore the names of *Le Toron des Chevalier* (Tower of the Knights) and *Castellum bonu Latronis* (Fortress of the Good Thief). The main building is the old Tegart police fort, from the British Mandate. Built in 1943, it was used, ironically, as a prison housing, among others, members of *Haganah*. During the War of Independence, there was a futile series of attempts to capture it, with the IDF finally taking it from Jordan, in 1967. It includes one of the world's finest armor museums and the Wall of Names Memorial, featuring the names of over 4,800 fallen Armored Corps soldiers. Although its primary focus is on the Armored Corps, it does feature self-propelled artillery including unique weapons based on the Sherman.

The ***Israeli Air Force Museum*** is located on the grounds of Hatzerim Air Base, southwest of Be'er Sheva, seen here in the background, in the Negev Desert. Its focus is, of course, on the many types of aircraft used by the IAF. Among its varied exhibits are a Spitfire, a P-51 Mustang, several *Kfirs* and the Boeing 707 that was used as a flying command post during the famous Entebbe rescue mission. For our purposes here, there are also vehicles and anti-aircraft artillery used by the IAF. Interestingly enough, during my 1999 visit, the female airman at the ticket window was a reservist, whose family residence was in Silver Spring, MD, in the US, and she attended my *alma mater*, the University of Maryland.

1 In the Beginning

Acquiring artillery

Members of the Jewish Settlement Police (*Misteret Ha'Yishuvim Ha'Iviryim*) practice with a small ex-British 2-inch (51mm) mortar in Kfar Yeladim in the northern Galilee region. The JSP was generously equipped, by the British, including uniforms and weapons. (Zoltan Kluger, Israeli Government Press Office)

The *Napoleonchik* (Little Napoleon), likely nicknamed by a recent French immigrant to Israel, was the French-built *Canon de 65M (Montagne) Modele 1906 Schneider-Ducrest*. It could be towed or broken down, carried by mules or horses. Having no real gun sights, they were aimed, more or less over the barrel. Initially, the cash-strapped *Haganah* acquired only three guns, but they later supplemented them with 35 more. The first of these were initially shipped from Europe on the *SS Borea*, hidden under other cargo. Received on May 15, 1948, after being delayed by the Royal Navy, they were used extensively in the War of Independence, beginning early in the conflict with the soon-to-be IDF's very first documented use of field artillery at Degania. Later, they were used against the Jordanians at Latrun and against the Egyptians in the Negev.

Degania is a *kibbutz* on the shore of Lake Kinneret (Biblical Sea of Galilee), just below the Jordan River. It was established in 1910 and by 1948 there were actually two *kibbutzim*, *Alef* (A) and *Bet* (B), several hundred yards apart (Degania *Gimel* (C) was disbanded in 1929). On 20 May 1948, six days after Israel's Declaration of Independence and six days prior to the official establishment of the Israel Defense Force, a company of Syrian infantry, five ex-French *Renault* R35 tanks and several armored cars, along with ex-French *Automilitailleuse* Dodge 4x2s (with the nickname *Tanake)*, attacked Degania *Alef*. An additional two infantry companies and nine R35s attacked Degania *Bet*. Both settlements were defended by local militia and units of *Hativat Carmeli* (later designated as the IDF's 2nd *'Carmeli'* Brigade). After the tanks were repulsed at Degania *Alef* by *Molotov*

It is very appropriate to include this homemade mortar, outside of a clandestine *Haganah* workshop near Tel Aviv. The timeframe is May 1948, so there are some real mortars and artillery arriving or already in the *Yishuv*. However, what can be more appropriate for a book about Sherman-based SP artillery than showing a picture of a mortar on Sherman road wheels? (Frank Shershel, Israeli Government Press Office)

Cocktails and a PIAT anti-tank weapon, the remaining Syrian forces at Degania *Bet* were surprised by the fire from a battery of four *Napoleonchik* howitzers on the Alumot-Poriyya Ridge to the north-west. At the time, they were so new to the Israelis that the crews fired some practice rounds into the lake before turning the guns on the Syrians. One of the subsequent rounds hit an ammunition supply dump, setting off a frightening series of explosions. Shortly afterward, the Syrians retreated, leaving behind several tanks. The Israelis then proceeded to capture the Arab village of Zema, to the north-east. One of the *R35*s remains at Degania today, right where it was left back then, as a monument to the defenders.

Another famous artillery piece acquired, and used effectively in 1948 was the *Krupp* 75mm (7.5 cm) Model 1903 field gun. It is best known in the IDF for being used in the direct-fire role against a combined force of Iraqi-Sudanese-Egyptian troops in the Faluja Pocket, an area now occupied by the town of Kiryat Gat, about 35 miles (56 kilometers) south of Tel Aviv. Kiryat Gat was founded in 1954. It was named after the ancient Philistine city of Gath, hometown of Goliath (of David vs. Goliath fame). Although withdrawn from active service during the 1950s, it was used extensively for training. There are reports, unconfirmed by absolute photographic evidence at this time, that several (perhaps six?) of the 32 de-militarized M4 (105) (British designation: Sherman IA) tanks, acquired in Italy in the fall of 1948, were temporarily fitted with these weapons, pending the availability of more appropriate guns.

In addition to standard field artillery, the young IDF began acquiring anti-tank guns, anti-aircraft guns, mortars of all kinds and eventually recoilless rifles and rockets, albeit several decades for the latter. The more identifiable anti-tank guns included the British QF (**Q**uick **F**iring) 6-pounder and QF 17-pounder, along with the French *CN-90-F1/DEFA*.

The IDF used a wide variety of mortars, ranging in size from 50–60mm, 81mm to the heavy 120mm and 160mm. Some were captured in combat, while others were purchased abroad by the aforementioned acquisition teams. Soltam Systems, Ltd. manufactured 120mm and 160mm types, locally.

Artillery support for *PALMACH* and the newly-established Israel Defense Force (IDF) was initially limited to obsolete or improvised weapons. Nicknamed *Napoleonchik* (Little Napoleon) by Israeli troops, this French 65mm howitzer, officially known as *Canon de 65M (Montagne) Modele 1906 Schneider-Ducrest*, was designed to support operations in difficult terrain. It could be towed or broken down into pieces and carried by pack mule. Assigned to *Hativat Har'el (Hativat* = Brigade), these two *PALMACHniks*, Moshe Mottola and Ethan (no surname given) stand by their *Napoleonchik* in the hills surrounding Jerusalem. (*PALMACH* Photo Gallery)

Anti-aircraft (AA) artillery in IDF service is often overlooked, particularly during the earlier years. However, a number of such weapons were used during the early conflicts. These included small-caliber machine guns, 20mm guns and weapons like the 40mm *Bofors* and the ex-British 3.7-inch AA gun. The latter was roughly equivalent to the infamous German 88mm AA gun. However, unlike that weapon, it was not used in the anti-tank or field artillery role. According to a veteran of the regular 402 Battalion, his unit did make use of a 30mm AA gun adapted to a direct-fire role against Syrian bunkers. They nicknamed that gun *Sayeret Netz* (Reconnaissance Hawk).

Similarly named, yet unrelated in any way, the American-built HAWK (**H**oming **A**ll the **W**ay **K**iller) system appeared in the 1970s, ushering in the AA missile era. Initially, the Artillery Corps used anti-aircraft weapons, but the Israeli Air Force (IAF) now controls them.

As with most modern armies, the IDF recognized early on that self-propelled artillery would be needed to keep pace with, and to support, armored units during mobile combat. The first of these entered service as early as 1948, as rudimentary conversions on American-built half-tracks. Vehicles armed with 6-pounder anti-tank guns and turreted 20mm guns supplemented the few available tanks in providing an armored element for the fledgling IDF. Later, the 90mm *DEFA* and the *SS11* anti-tank missile, also of French origin, 81mm and 120mm mortars were mounted in half-tracks. Airborne and scout units used jeep-mounted American M40A1 recoilless rifles and the modern TOW (**T**ube-launched, **O**ptically-tracked, **W**ire-guided) missile system. Shorter-lived in service were jeeps and light trucks armed with the *SS10* and the Soviet-built *Sagger*. Relatively unknown, the Nord Aviation *SS10* was a wire-guided missile used in 1956, mounted on Dodge-built ¾-Ton Weapons Carriers. A few other weapons will be covered in later chapters, as they pertain to their respective Sherman platforms.

This *Napoleonchik* is being used in the assault on Be'er Sheva in October 1948. This pre-World War I weapon was first used in combat against Syrian forces, during the battle for Degania, on 20 May 1948. Subsequently, it was also prominent at Kiryat-Gat, near Gaza, and in the unsuccessful assault against the Jordanians at Latrun. Eventually, a total of 38 of these weapons saw service. Note the lack of a sighting mechanism, requiring the crew to sight it over the barrel. (Hugo Mendelson, Israeli Government Press Office)

This gun commander is about to give the order to fire. The small size is very evident in this view. Be'er Sheva is located in the Negev Desert, which is also very evident in this photograph. However, portions of the Negev are also used for farming. Note the tents, which mean that this position was occupied for some time. (Hugo Mendelson, Israeli Government Press Office)

Although this photograph is not of the highest quality, it does very clearly show the extent of the barren landscape. This battery of *Napoleonchiks* was quiet, during a lull in the fighting, but the crews are now preparing for action. The four guns are dispersed in a semi-circular pattern to achieve a wide range of fire. (Hugo Mendelson, Israeli Government Press Office)

This howitzer and its crew were photographed during a training session in the summer of 1948. The British were indeed, a major supplier of uniforms and weapons before and during the War of Independence. Some material was provided deliberately as part of co-operation between *Haganah*, the various Jewish police units and the British Army. At the same time, other items were clandestinely 'appropriated', and other material was 'rescued' from dump sites when the British withdrew. Note that the helmets worn here include both the Mk.I, known as the 'Brodie' helmet, and the mid-World War II Mk.III, on the left. (*PALMACH* Photo Gallery, *Gachal* Album)

Several of these historic howitzers are on display today, with this one outside the main building at *Beit Ha'Totchan* (Gunner's House or House of Artillerymen), site of the Artillery Corps Memorial and Museum, in the picturesque northern Israeli town of Zichron Ya'akov. (Joshua Weingarten)

Interestingly enough, this much better preserved example is displayed a long way from *Beit Ha'Totchan*, in Yad Mordechai. This *kibbutz* was the scene of a significant battle on 19–24 May 1948, that delayed the Egyptian advance, although the enemy was eventually successful. In November, the IDF succeeded in re-capturing the *kibbutz*, an action during which this gun may have been used. (Joshua Weingarten)

This one is part of the War of Independence Memorial in the city of Tiberias. Interestingly enough, Tiberias sits on the shore of Lake Kinneret (Biblical Sea of Galilee), not too far from Degania *Alef* and *Bet*, site of the first Israeli use of this weapon. It is very well preserved, even as it sits exposed to the weather. The author had the opportunity to visit Tiberias, with friend Joe Prisco, in 1999. From a boat tour on the lake, the nearby *Ramat Ha'Golan* (Golan Heights) is an imposing sight. (Dr. Avishai Teicher, PikiWiki Israel)

Another ancient weapon used in the War of Independence was the British QF (Quick Firing) 3.7-inch Mountain gun. This World War I antique is shown here, with soldiers from *Hativat Yiftach*, a *PALMACH* brigade originally assigned to the center of the *Yishuv*. Later, it moved south, to the Be'er Sheva area, where this photograph was taken. Note the female *PALMACHnik*, as well as her male counterpart on the right, still wearing what looks like his *kalpak*, a woolen or fur busby, worn by the *Notrim*. (*PALMACH* Photo Gallery)

Another acquisition team managed to purchase 32 relatively inexpensive howitzers in Mexico. The French-built 75mm *Saint Chamond-Mondragon* was called *Cucaracha* (cockroach, although an Israeli source says it was named after the song) by Mexican troops, so that name carried over into IDF service. When they arrived in country, in September, they were not exactly battle-worthy, so a lot of work was needed to prepare them for that service. (872 Battalion Unit History)

This rare and slightly scratched photograph shows a battery of *Cucarachas* in action in the Negev. The timing could be during *Mivtza* (Operation) *Yo'av* (Operation Ten Plagues, a Biblical reference to the Egyptian opponents), during the battles for Be'er Sheva in late October. The lack of cold-weather clothing discounts the offensive against the Egyptian Army that began on December 22, *Mivtza Horev*. This particular battery had several *MACHALniks* in it, with two South Africans, Melville Malkin and Hillel Daleski, servicing this howitzer. (Defense Establishment Archives)

There are several 75mm *Saint Chamond-Mondragon* howitzers on display in Israel. This one is at *Batey Haosef*, otherwise known as the IDF Collection Houses, in Tel Aviv-Yafo (Jaffa). Located just a few blocks from the beach, it may one day, according to rumors, be closed to make room for real estate development. Note the date on the placard, 1903, indicating its pre-World War I lifespan. (Joshua Weingarten)

When weapons and vehicles arrived, first in Mandatory Palestine (referred to by Jews as the *Yishuv* – Settlement of Jews) and then in Israel, the first thing to be done was a detailed inspection. After this, time was needed to service them to varying degrees, to ensure that they would function on the battlefield. In this case, in March 1948, technicians are servicing the barrels for the newly-arrived *Saint Chamond-Mondragon* howitzers. Weapons and vehicles were difficult to come by, and sometimes a low price paid for them would be offset by the amount of work necessary to refurbish them. However, the exceptional skill of Jewish ordnance technicians, and their prior experience in other countries, allowed for the Jews in Palestine/Israel to make the most of what they did have. (Israeli Government Press Office)

These men are re-assembling an unidentified cannon carriage in March 1948. Given the spoked wooden wheels and so forth, this is obviously one of the more aged weapons. Comparing it to the previous photos, this is not a *Cucaracha*. (Israeli Government Press Office)

Batey Haosef is a repository for all sorts of weapons used by Israel and its enemies over the years. This is a sampling of the motley collection of old artillery pieces used in 1948. Note the carriages with wooden wheels. At the corner is a *Canon de 105 mle 1913 Schneider*, a Franco-Russian design from the early 1900s, used in both World Wars by several countries. Next to it, minus its shield, is a British QF (**Q**uick **F**iring) 3.7-inch Mountain Gun, first used in 1917. Third in line to the left is the *Cucaracha*. The last antique in line is a *Canon de 75mm Modele 1897*. The first and last of these guns were retrofitted with rubber tires for use in World War II.

Armies have always found ways to deceive an enemy regarding their relative strength, or lack thereof. Here, these *PALMACH*niks have just what they need, a wooden cannon. From a distance, with this fake gun dug in somewhere, it could be enough to divert someone's attention. As a humorous side comment, is the soldier with his hand tucked into his shirt with a fake 'hat', paying homage to Napoleon? (*PALMACH* Photo Gallery)

While this photo is not the best quality, it does show a very rare cannon in Artillery Corps use. Compare this weapon with the one on the corner in the photograph on the previous page from *Batey Haosef*. It is the *Canon de 105 mle 1913 Schneider.* According to the original caption, it was assigned to *Hativat Har'el*, originally assigned to the Central Front before moving south to fight the Egyptians. Note the winter clothing which is appropriate for *Mivtza Horev* in the winter of 1948–1949. Today, this brigade, later known as the 10th *'Har'el'* Armored Brigade, is honored with a monument on top of *Har Adar* (Radar hill), not far from Latrun and Jerusalem. (*PALMACH* Photo Gallery)

For a period of time after Independence, the new IDF and the *PALMACH* were somewhat estranged. Consequently, some *TZAHAL* brigades were already formed before the integration of *PALMACH* troops and their existing units. Thus, *Hativat Yitach*, formed from three *PALMACH* battalions, became the 11th *'Yiftach'* Brigade. This unit began its service in the central region, but it eventually transferred to the south where it participated in *Mivtza Yo'av* in October. The location and timing for this photograph is 'identified' by its reference to *Hativat Yiftach,* the desolate terrain and the warm clothing required at times in October, even in the desert. The field piece is a *Krupp* 75mm Model 1903. (Public Domain, Album of *Hativat* (Brigade) *Yiftach*)

This photograph is dated January 1949, which marks this *Krupp* 75mm crew as participating in *Mivtza Horev*, another Biblical reference, this time to the old Hebrew name for Mount Sinai (now called Jebel Musa, Arabic for 'Mount of Moses'). Note the uniforms which are definitely ex-British. The sweaters also confirm the timing for Operation *Horev*, which extended into the winter of 1949. Note also that the gun layer is adjusting his scope before opening the small hatch in the shield. Crewmen wear the 'Brodie' helmet, as well as the Mk.III, from 1943. (*PALMACH* Photo Gallery)

This *Krupp* 75 crew is also dressed warmly, including British-style sweaters and Mk.I 'Brodie' helmets. Once again, the terrain suggests the Negev in the winter of 1948–1949. During the War of Independence, these weapons still had spoked wooden wheels dating back to World War I. (Public Domain, IDF Encyclopedia)

This *Krupp* 75 gun was seen here in April 1950. A battery of them is being used during a ceremony honoring artillery soldiers who fell during the War of Independence. Note that the crew positions were distinctly British in arrangement, which was typical of the early IDF. A number of *Haganah/PALMACH* soldiers had served in the Jewish Brigade of the British Army during World War II, plus many *MACHAL*niks had military experience, bringing the skills learned into the young IDF. (Fritz Cohen, Israeli Government Press Office)

On the other hand, for the sake of comparison, these artillerymen are dressed for warm weather, once again in British uniforms. The terrain still suggests the Negev, but it was 10 September 1951. IDF maneuvers were often held in this area, and still are today. Note the gun number '57' on the shield. Also, noted on the shield in Hebrew, 'Towing Speed 40 KPH (**K**ilometers **p**er **H**our) and Tire Pressure 40 pounds'. By this time, the *Krupp* guns were refitted with rubber tires. (Teddy Brauner, Israeli Government Press Office)

This is the same battery during the autumn maneuvers in 1951. A careful look at the American-made GMC trucks in each photo will confirm that it was the same vehicle grouping. Note the open sighting door and the gun number, this time on the rear of the shield. (Teddy Brauner, Israeli Government Press Office)

This battery of *Krupp* 75s is participating in the Tel Aviv Independence Day parade in May 1952. Thanks to the miracle of satellite imagery and 'street views', using the building in the background, which is still there, the exact location is at the intersection of Allenby Street, the parade route itself, and Sheinkin Street, to the left, and King George Street, out of sight to the far left, near present-day *Magen David* Square. *Magen David* translates as Star of David in the USA (or Shield of David to our Anglo-Saxon brethren). The prime movers are Canadian-made CMP (Canadian Military Pattern) trucks. Given the constant threat of war or other violence, the Israeli public have always been interested in military parades or exhibitions, with the corresponding sense of security. These parades, the last of which was in 1973, were always well-attended. Prior to 1973, the parades alternated between the major cities. (Public Domain, Central Zionist Archives)

In this photograph, crews prepare to fire the *Krupp* 75 during a demonstration at Ramat Gan Stadium on Independence Day, 1956. During the celebrations in 1956, the main IDF parade was in Haifa. Note the mortar in the background, indicating that other weapons are displayed as well. (Fritz Cohen, Israeli Government Press Office)

At yet another artillery demonstration in September of the same year, a group of *Krupp* 75s is shown being deployed in the same stadium in Ramat Gan, a former *moshav* turned major city. The crewmen wore helmets on this occasion. The uniforms and equipment, including the web gear, were all of British design. (Fritz Cohen, Israeli Government Press Office)

On the same day, an infantry unit marched past the artillery display. Shown, from left to right, are WC-51 ¾-ton prime movers, most likely for the *Krupp* field guns, six *Krupp* 75mm cannons, six 120mm towed mortars and a row of QF 6-pounder anti-tank guns. Crews stand by in front of each weapon. (Fritz Cohen, Israeli Government Press Office)

In this broader view of the same formation are a row of six *Hispano-Suiza* 20mm anti-aircraft guns and, off to the side, some QF 25-pounders. Of additional interest are the two *Napoleonchiks* on the track. (Fritz Cohen, Israeli Government Press Office)

At the conclusion of the artillery portion of this display, after all other guns except the *Napoleonchik* have left, the battery of four 25-pounders fired a salute. (Fritz Cohen, Israeli Government Press Office)

A number of *Krupp* field guns are displayed in town squares, intersections and museums around Israel. Such widespread use of this gun for monuments simply illustrates its importance in IDF Artillery Corps history. This one is at *Ha'Totchan,* where the displays sit along wooded trails and among the trees themselves. Even at this late date, the tires have different tread patterns.

This is the exhibit at *Batey Haosef,* where it shares space with many weapons from both sides of the various Arab-Israeli wars and campaigns. Note the two vision ports with closed hatches. The date of 1917 may be confused with a British 75mm gun.

This gun is displayed at the *Beit Ha'Gdudim* Museum, honoring the World War I Jewish Legion in *Moshav* Avichail, near the city of Netanya between Tel Aviv and Haifa. The gun is still there today although the barrel rests in full recoil, due to an empty cylinder. (Moshe Pridan, Israeli Government Press Office)

Rishon Le'Zion is a city just south of Tel Aviv, noted for being the second Jewish settlement in the *Yishuv*, behind Petach Tikva. This *Krupp 75* is part of a monument to city residents who died fighting for Israel. Other similar displays are scattered around the country, but space here is limited. (Fritz Cohen, Israeli Government Press Office)

Another rarely-seen IDF artillery piece was the British World War I-era QF 18-pounder which was the backbone of the Royal Artillery during that conflict. It was actually one of the foundation weapons whose design prompted the development of the QF 25-pounder. This relaxed and smiling group poses with an 18-pounder in Acre, after its capture by *Hativat Carmeli* in May 1948. Acre is north of Haifa, near the coast, hence the evergreen trees. These troops from *Carmeli*'s 22nd Battalion are dressed in British-style uniforms, including paratroop helmets. Note the Sten Guns, which could be ex-British, or they may be locally-manufactured. Also, note the female soldier in the front row. At one point, *PALMACH* had over 1,600 female members. (University of Haifa, YSN Collection)

The first QF (**Q**uick **F**iring) 25-pounder field gun/howitzer was acquired clandestinely in 1948. *Haganah* members, disguised as British soldiers and under the command of an Australian, the former Major Mike Scott, tricked a British officer into releasing a 25-pounder as an alleged replacement for one damaged in an accident. It was used during the first assault on Latrun. Others were acquired later, and they were used extensively in 1956 and 1967. While the crew looks very British in appearance, the rifle is a German *Mauser 98K*. The Hebrew lettering on the soldier's overalls reads 'Number 1', so the question is does that refer to this first of many gun-howitzers to come? Interesting. (Public Domain)

This battery of 25-pounders is preparing for an exercise or a demonstration somewhere in Israel, on December 7, 1948. It would be a huge, yet interesting stretch of the imagination, to say that perhaps the celebration was for what Americans refer to as Pearl Harbor Day, marking the US entry into World War II, and the ultimate defeat of the Nazi regime and the end of the *Shoah* (Holocaust). The crews wear olive drab British-style uniforms and berets. Note that two guns are missing their muzzle brakes. (Israeli Government Press Office)

Haifa hosted a Liberation Day parade on April 19, 1949. Part of the celebrations involved a demonstration of IDF artillery strength, including this QF 25-pounder. As was typical of the early years for the IDF, this crew wore a mix of gear, including British-style sweaters, but they had American-style helmets and webbing. (Teddy Brauner, Israeli Government Press Office)

This is a training exercise in November 1954, with a relatively unusual (in Israeli service) limber/gun combination. The crew is outfitted completely in ex-British uniforms and gear. The rifles, however, are what appear to be *Mauser 98Ks* apparently, the rifle of choice for a number of years, even seen in use in 1967. Of course, there were other bolt-action rifles in use including the American Springfield, but the *Mauser* was the most common, by far. Note that the gun shield bore a full registration number, including the Hebrew letter *tsaldi*. This was actually a prefix to the number, since Hebrew words are read from right to left, while numbers are read from left to right. (Israeli Government Press Office)

This example is in use during the Sinai Campaign in 1956. In Israeli parlance, this war was known as *Mivtza Kadesh*. It was a joint effort with the British and French, called Operation *Musketeer*, intended to force Egypt to re-open the Suez Canal by actually taking control of it, and to lift their blockade of Eilat and the Straights of Tiran. Note the early uniforms and headgear worn by the crew. A large turntable beneath the gun allowed for 360-degree traverse. Note also how the tires sit on the base. (Defense Establishment Archives)

In the IDF, as in many military organizations, graduation or 'passing-out' ceremonies, are important and extravagant affairs. In this case, the 'passing-out' of artillery cadets on December 11, 1956 includes a salute by a battery equipped with QF 25-pounder gun/howitzers. Note the British-style uniforms, bolt-action rifles and the stenciling on the gun shield. (Israeli Government Press Office)

Political ceremonies also featured units of the IDF. At the inauguration of President Ben Zvi, outside the *Knesset* (Hebrew for 'The Gathering') building in Jerusalem, November 1957, this unit of 25-pounders was prepared to fire its salute. Even a ceremony as important as this did not prevent one citizen from hanging laundry on their balcony, visible on the building to the right, just above the muzzle brake! Life goes on. (David Gurfinkel, Israeli Government Press Office)

The 25-pounder was still in widespread use during the Six-Day War in 1967. This photograph shows a crew involved in sustained fire against Syrian positions on the Golan Heights. Note the stack of shells within easy reach. The turntable is lowered, allowing for 360-degree traverse, by raising and turning the trail. The wheels rest on the turntable, easily 'riding' it during the turn. (Defense Establishment Archives)

Batey Haosef has an excellent intact display. The metal plaque identifies the weapon with its introduction into service date, 1941. Note how the gun sight aperture swings open for the gun layer. The turntable hinges show how it was dropped to the ground, after which the crew would pull it into place.

The gun/howitzer displayed at *Beit Ha'Totchan* is missing its turntable. The 'gun/howitzer' refers to its use in both the direct-fire and plunging-fire roles. In World War II, the British often used it as an emergency anti-tank gun. There was also a version of this carriage in British service with a 17-pounder gun. It is an excellent piece, in a beautiful and serene setting. Normally, red or black paint is used to identify areas requiring regular maintenance, which is not the case here. Even today, people with whom I have spoken, still believe Israel to be a desert. Obviously, this is not true. (Photo above, Eran Kaufman. Photo below, David 'Didi' Levy)

2 Israeli M7 Priest

Logical choice of platform

The newly-acquired Priests were delivered in late 1960, via the Port of Haifa. This photograph shows two of them being loaded onto a railroad flatcar. The engine deck cannot be seen but it is assumed that the M4-style front portion was added in Israel for standardization, as well as additional protection from debris. (Defense Establishment Archives)

Following the War of Independence, neighboring Arab countries expanded their armed forces. To counter this growth, which included new and more modern weapons, most, but not all of which were provided by the Soviet Union with its corresponding presumed threat of more imminent conflict, the IDF expanded as well. Planners quickly recognized the need for a larger armored component, with the corresponding need for supporting mobile artillery. France was one of the few countries willing to supply weapons to Israel, so that was a logical place to go. The French government was anxious to expand its military exports, having recently produced its first locally-designed modern tank, the *AMX*-13. Having already recognized the need for corresponding mobile pieces of artillery to support tanks, they also produced the *60 Obusier Auto-Moteur de 105 Modele 50*, a 105mm howitzer with limited traverse in a fixed casemate, built on that AMX-13 chassis. As a result, the IDF acquired its first self-propelled gun on a tank hull.

The pre-eminent tank in IDF use during this time was the M4 Sherman series, various models of which entered service in increasing numbers during the 1950s. As was the case with the United States during World War II, the logical choice of platform for self-propelled artillery was, therefore, the Sherman. Although many of the base tanks were re-built and upgraded vehicles obtained from scrap yards around the globe, complete and serviceable tanks and towed/self-propelled artillery were also purchased directly from France. Consequently, in addition to the aforementioned *AMX*-13-

As with every other major military force, *TZAHAL* quickly learned that self-propelled artillery was necessary in order to support tank units and fast-moving infantry. One of the earliest vehicles is totally unrelated to the Sherman, but it is interesting. This photo was taken on May 5, 1962, during the Independence Day Parade in Tel Aviv. Research turned up several different descriptions, but I will go with *Automoteur de 105 du AMX en Casemate*, which is also mentioned, *en Anglais*, as the *AMX*-105A Mk 61. These guns were used through the Six-Day War. (Fritz Cohen, Israeli Government Press Office)

based 105mm howitzer, France also provided the first of the next generation of IDF self-propelled artillery.

As early as October 1955, the IDF Deputy Chief of Staff expressed an interest in obtaining at least 40 M7 Priest self-propelled howitzers. It was not until 1960, however, that the IDF actually purchased its first Priests from France, enough to eventually equip three full battalions.

Service with the IDF actually began shortly after their delivery, likely in early 1961, beginning with training and orientation. By March 1963, 12 Priests were deployed with the regular 404 (without a 'th') Battalion of the IDF Artillery Corps. Additional Priests equipped the reserve 822 Battalion and the reserve 827 Battalion.

When placed in service with the Artillery Corps, these M7 Priests differed considerably in appearance from the original production version. The engine decks were modified, as with most other Shermans in IDF service at the time, to have a modified version of the radial-engine style of armored cover for the forward engine deck air vent. It is important to remember that, unlike many other Sherman tanks and variants in Israeli service, the M7 already had the Continental R975 radial engine. For the sake of clarification, the model designation of 'M7A1' is often used, incorrectly, to identify vehicles with the upswept return rollers or other later visual features . In fact, it was the official designation for similar vehicles based on the M4A3 with its Ford V8 engine, plus the engine deck and rear of that series. Also, they were fitted with direct-fire gun sights identical to those on Sherman turrets, and a gun travel lock at the front. In all other respects, they were simply intermediate production versions, standardized to include the heavy-duty Sherman-style suspension bogies and cast FDAs (**F**inal **D**rive **A**ssembly) of either style. They also featured retro-fitted folding side armor plates which had been originally welded in place on many Priests during World War II. Note: the reader should also understand that the name 'Priest' was given to the series by the British, following their practice of naming SP guns with ecclesiastic-type verbiage, such as the World War II Bishop and the post-war Abbot.

All three units fought in the Six-Day War in 1967, normally in the indirect fire mode, as expected. However, at least one vehicle did engage Egyptian tanks, destroying a T-34/85 with direct fire. This encounter is a prime example of the fluid nature of combat, and the need for mobile artillery in support of armored units. June 9 was the third day of combat, with the 822 Battalion in support of General Avraham Yoffe's reserve armor. Having already defeated the Egyptian forces at Jebel Libni (one of the Egyptian Air Force's forward airfields in the northern Sinai, south-west of El Arish, bombed on the war's first day), Yoffe was headed toward Bir Hassneh. At this point, his units were effectively cutting off the Egyptian retreat toward the Mitla Pass. Suddenly, a T-34/85 from the Egyptian 3rd Division carrying retreating Egyptian infantry, approached a column of Priests and half-tracks from the 822 as it traveled down the road. Machine-gun fire from the lead half-track quickly eliminated the tank-borne infantry. Then, a Priest hastily fired a 105mm HE round, which missed. Fortunately, the battery *KA'AT* (Hebrew acronym identifying the gunnery officer) climbed aboard the Priest after jumping from his half-track. Sighting through the barrel in the absence of a true direct-fire sight, he fired an anti-tank round, striking the T-34 and causing it to burn. A second AT round was fired for good measure, and the column then continued on its way.

After the Six-Day War, the Priests continued to serve. The 404 Battalion remained in position near the Canal where it transitioned to self-propelled 155mm howitzers, before participating in the fiercely-fought artillery duels of the War of Attrition. In one such action involving a different Priest unit, on July 24, 1969, near the road from Gidi Pass, four Egyptian aircraft attacked a Priest-equipped battery from, once again, 822 Battalion while they were engaged in an artillery duel. One of the Priest crewmen, Shaia Rotshtein, tried to engage the aircraft, with his vehicle's .50-caliber M2HB (**H**eavy **B**arrel) heavy machine gun, but he ran out of ammunition and was killed before he could reload. Two of the Priests were destroyed, with photos of one of them shown later, but the remaining vehicles moved to another location and continued the fight. Actions like this continued in an exhausting campaign for the artillerymen, until the official end of the War of Attrition, on August 7, 1970.

Also during the War of Attrition, as mentioned, 404 Battalion had dropped its Priests, which subsequently went to the reserve 829 Battalion. This latter unit then joined the other two Priest units to fight on the *Ramat Ha'Golan* (Golan Heights) during the *Yom Kippur* War. The action on the Golan was so intense that many of the howitzers were fired until the barrels simply burned out.

Finally, in 1974, the M7 Priests were withdrawn from active IDF service. While they were no longer 'active' as mobile weapons. Though essentially gone, they were not quite forgotten, however.

Shortly after the *Yom Kippur* War, the commander of the Northern Command, Rafael Eitan, recognized a need for local defense of *kibbutzim* and *moshavim* along the northern borders. Realizing that there was still sufficient 105mm ammunition for the recently deactivated Priests, he decided to include them in his plans for *HAGMAR* (a Hebrew acronym for 'regional

The first unit equipped with the new Priests was the regular 404 Battalion. These newly-issued vehicles were photographed in the Negev in 1961, as the crews became familiar with them. Although the photograph is of less-than-optimum quality, it does show that these Priests appear to be darker in color, most likely the French brownish olive drab, which would be appropriate for that year. (Oded Bonneh)

In this photograph, taken in late 1961 or early 1962, the Priests' lower hulls are covered in dust, while the howitzer barrels are still dark. The half-track is an unmodified M2A1 with what could be a covered Besa machine gun. The one in the background is most likely an IHC-built M5. Neither one gives any indication that it was equipped to function as a *MAPIK*, an armored vehicle used by the Fire-Control Team. These Priests were also not yet fitted with the gun travel lock. (Oded Bonneh)

defense'). Ten vehicles were initially modified for use in this role as dug-in artillery support for the various settlements. The engines were removed and the engine bay was used for storage. However, the project met with some resistance over concern for having the howitzers manned by inexperienced or untrained people, particularly in the indirect-fire role.

To test the idea, two Priests were deployed at *Kibbutz* Kinneret near Tiberias and its 'twin' *Moshav* Kinneret, aimed toward the Jordan passes. The Artillery Corps prepared and taught a training course for the villagers who would man them. Most of these villagers were older reservists, many of retirement age, with no artillery experience. Even with the problem of being unable to actually conduct live-fire from these positions, and after much hard and dedicated work by the reservists, the training program was ultimately considered to be a success. The importance of local defense forces like this was such that the first group's graduation ceremony was even attended by future Prime Minister Shimon Peres, then Defense Minister.

Eventually, 10 pairs of Priests were deployed, with the vehicles emplaced with a predetermined field of fire toward the front, along with permanent aiming stakes set in concrete. To promote proficiency, the Artillery Corps conducted periodic refresher courses for the crews and inspections for the weapons, until the whole program eventually fell into disuse.

These local defenses were quite extensive in some cases, reminiscent of the larger fortifications on the Golan Heights' Purple Line and the Sinai's Bar Lev Line, including trench systems, mortar and machine gun pits and all of the relevant ammunition storage. Besides the Priests, the primary weapons systems employed for other *kibbutzim* and *moshavim* included a number of redundant M-50 tanks, a few captured T-34/85 tanks, concrete pillboxes with M1 cupolas from M48 tanks, a few turrets from obsolete armored cars, and so on. In addition to the northern borders with Lebanon and Syria, similar defenses were constructed along the Jordan River Valley, known today as the Occupied Territories or West Bank.

The 1963 Independence Day parade in Haifa maybe one of the newly-acquired Priests' earliest public appearances. A careful look at this vehicle reveals a registration number 270152 and that, by now, the vehicles were painted sand gray. There is some photographic evidence of other IDF vehicles, that this first lighter color was somewhat yellowish, rather than grayish. Note the hinged side panel behind the pulpit. As built, this vehicle was without protection in this area, exposing the tops of the ammunition tubes. During World War II, the US Army authorized the addition of armor plate welded in place. Subsequently though, the welds were broken, and hinges were added. (Moshe Pridan, Israeli Government Press Office)

The greater part of an unidentified battalion's Priests is seen here in the same parade. Tool and spare track stowage varied considerably from the former American version. For instance, instead of a pick-axe head on the vehicle's right, American M7s carried an individual track link in an open sheet metal bin. Also, the other spare track links were in similar bins, on the left. Interestingly enough, although the spare tracks were new, the vehicle rides on worn T48 rubber chevron tracks, probably to protect the paving on the road. (Moshe Pridan, Israeli Government Press Office)

Independence Day parades were an excellent means for the IDF to showcase its weaponry. This 1964 event was in Be'ersheva and the unit appears to be a reserve battalion. Note that the vehicles are fitted with different types of tracks. The first M7, which is also the one seen in the second close-up photo, has what is often too quickly identified as the T54E1 steel chevron type, when, in fact, they are the post-war T74 style. The most noticeable differences are the small metal protrusions on the edges of the plate of the T54E1, which are not here. However, in the original image for the second photo, one can see that the spare links are, indeed, T54E1s. The next several have much-worn rubber chevron T48 tracks. Altogether, 11 Priests are visible. (Fritz Cohen, Israeli Government Press Office)

This Priest brings up the rear of the unit, with the track of the vehicle in front barely visible, on the right. This vehicle seems to be fully modified, including the commander's gun sight just visible in the front of him. Note the Dodge ¾-ton WC-series medium truck behind the Priest. Note also the palm trees, making the parade route most likely to be *Ha'Haganah* Avenue, along the beach.

The following year, in 1965, the parade was in Tel Aviv. This aerial photograph shows several artillery units in a staging area prior to the event. From the bottom, there is a mortar unit with both towed and self-propelled weapons. Visible are six towed Soltam-built 160mm mortars, 14 self-propelled *MACHMAT* 120mm mortars and one unarmed version. Next, there are 12 *TOMAT* M50 155mm SP howitzers, which constitute an entire battalion, with two half-tracks, possibly *MAPIKS*. The last artillery unit is a battalion of 12 Priests with four half-tracks. The half-tracks at the top cannot be definitively identified as to what type of unit is parked there. (Moshe Milner, Israeli Government Press Office)

Here the Priests pass in front of the reviewing stand at the 1965 Independence Day parade in Tel Aviv. The man in the light-colored suit is Prime Minister Levi Eshkol, and the officer to his left is one of his successors, the late Yitzak Rabin. The near vehicle is fitted with the smooth rubber block T51 tracks. Note that all of the vehicles are missing the armored visor for the driver. The lower hull is the riveted version used on the M3 (Lee/Grant series) and early M4 (Sherman I). Also, note the late final-drive assembly. This was a manufacturing feature of the last production batch in 1944. However, given the riveted lower hull, this one is more likely a later addition, similar to the manner in which most IDF M4A4s (Sherman V), all of which were built with the 3-piece FDA, came to be fitted with cast assemblies, of either type. (Fritz Cohen, Israeli Government Press Office)

This overhead view is from the same 1965 parade. Although the photograph was taken from a distance, the M4-style engine deck is just visible on the foreground vehicle. (Moshe Pridan, Israeli Government Press Office)

During the Six-Day War, Priest crews in the reserve battalions wore the older British World War I-style 'Brodie' helmet. This vehicle from the reserve 827 Battalion is shown on the Golan Heights, awaiting a firing mission. Note the hand-painted tactical markings. Remove those markings and, visually, this could be any Commonwealth unit in the Mediterranean theater in World War II. (Assaf Kutin, Israeli Government Press Office)

There were two reserve battalions equipped with Priests in 1967, 822 Battalion and 827 Battalion. 822 fought against the Egyptians, so, by process of elimination, 827 was the reserve Priest unit on the *Ramat Ha'Golan*. Another vehicle from 827 is seen here advancing on the Golan, on June 11. (Moshe Milner, Israeli Government Press Office)

This is an excellent view of the rear of an IDF Priest, also from 827 Battalion, in service. Note the exhaust deflector under the rear overhang, as well as the 'luggage rack'. (Moshe Milner, Israeli Government Press Office)

A battery of Priests from 827 Battalion fires against Syrian positions in 1967. The retrofit nature of the folding armor, with its relatively small hinges, can be seen clearly here. Note the manner in which the hinged armor follows the contour of the side armor plate. This is a feature of the retrofitted welded plates added in field depots during WWII. Note also the vertical weld on the hinged panel, indicating that it was fabricated from two pieces, a common practice by Ordnance Corps technicians when using armor plate cut from scrapyard vehicles. (Israeli Government Press Office)

822 Battalion is seen here after the Six-Day War. The location is Bir Tmadeh in the Sinai. The unit has just participated in a local victory parade. The M4-style engine deck from the Israeli upgrade is visible on the vehicle in the foreground. Also evident to some degree, are nearly all of the other external changes seen on IDF Priests, including the missing driver's armored visor, gun travel lock, Sherman gun sight, re-located tools and the spare track racks. Note that the travel locks are actually engaged, which is not a common sight in photographs. (Oded Bonneh)

The 1968 Independence Day parade, nearly a year after the Six-Day War, was held in Jerusalem. Perhaps to emphasize that the city was now united again, the route included Sultan Suleiman Street which is on the northern edge of the Arab Quarter of the Old City. In this photo, the Old City walls are likely to the right in the photo, near the Damascas Gate, not far from the Rockefeller Museum. At this time, the paint color is most likely a grayish sand, perhaps simply light gray, both of which are noticeable on existing vehicles. (Defense Establishment Archives)

As described in the text, an Egyptian air attack during the War of Attrition destroyed two Priests near the Canal in July 1969. This is one of them. At the time, the other two Priests in the battery moved to another location, leaving the wrecks behind. The T74 tracks, without the metal protrusions, are very clearly shown here. Note also, the Sherman commander's gun sight, above the driver's opening. (Oded Bonneh)

An intense fire burned off most of the paint, causing the metal to oxidize. This is a nice view of the rear deck, showing part of the M4-style air vent splashguard. The hinged side armor plates were blown completely off the vehicle. The vehicles with the M4-style deck addition to the forward section, did not have a hinged deck lid right behind it. Note the additional panel at the upper rear which is the so-called 'luggage rack', as seen on the tanks. (Oded Bonneh)

This was a staging area on the *Ramat Ha'Golan*, during the *Yom Kippur* War. Note the 160mm self-propelled mortar (discussed in Chapter 1 of Volume 2) behind the Priest, and the IHC (**I**nternational **H**arvester **C**orporation) half-track in the background. At this time, all three Priest battalions, 822, 827 and 829, were reserve units, and all three of them fought on the Syrian front. This proves that at least one of the IDF Priests had the deeper pulpit. This feature was added during the intermediate portion of the 1942/43 production run. The vehicle on the left has had its serial number painted out and moved to the FDA. (Defense Establishment Archives)

Color images of IDF Priests are rare, so this one is particularly interesting. The color is similar to that seen on other Shermans on the Egyptian Front in 1973. However, the Priest units all fought on the *Ramat Ha'Golan*. The M113 *Zelda* in the background points to a later timeframe, from the Six-Day War, so it is possible that this undated photo was taken during, or shortly after, the War of Attrition. Given an apparent lack of in-service type materials, this could also be in a storage yard prior to the implementation of *HAGMAR*. Under any circumstances, it is important to remember that IDF colors varied over time, between units, theaters of operations, and even because of the type of paint thinner used. (*Beit Ha'Totchan* Library, via an Artillery Corps veteran)

The Priests acquired from France were M7s that were manufactured with, or were upgraded with, some features common to the M4 Sherman series. This vehicle is fitted with the heavy duty M4 Sherman units, with the trailing return roller and raised roller mount, and its FDA (**F**inal **D**rive **A**ssembly) is the later Sherman version with the sharp contour. These were not standard until the final production run, so it is quite likely that these particular features are retrofits. As built, this Priest likely had the 3-piece FDA used on the M4 series without the cutout for the M3's sponson-mounted 75mm gun, seen on a few early vehicles.

From this angle, some other features indicate that this vehicle came from the initial batch. For instance, it has the riveted lower hull common to M3s and early M4s. It also has the non-standard armored flaps retrofitted to protect the ammunition bins. That these were once welded on, as part of a field retrofit during World War II, is evidenced by the contoured fit at the front of the panel. The 1944 production group had these hinged panels, as built, but they were not contoured to fit like this. The front and rear latches held the newly-hinged panel in place, with the one at the rear attaching to a post, added for this purpose. Note the weld mark on the folding panel.

The rear of the vehicle shows its lineage from the M3 series. Conversely, the M7B1 was distinguished by having the rear end and engine deck of the M4A3 (Sherman IV). Priests were equipped with the towing hitch for pulling an ammunition trailer, although the hitch itself is missing here.This vehicle is fitted with T74 type tracks.

The inset rear sponsons, taillights and the rear portion of the engine deck were all features of the Medium Tank M3. The 'luggage rack' was an added item. This visit to Zichron Ya'Akov was timed with the Memorial Day/Week celebrations in town which just happened to border *Beit Ha'Totchan*, thus the many flags. On this day, there was also a huge town party nearby.

From the front, the most distinguishing feature of the IDF Priest is the gun travel lock. Although common, this feature was not fitted universally. Note that it is mounted using extended bolts through the FDA. Also, tool stowage was re-positioned from the engine deck.

The engine deck is radically changed in appearance from the standard M7. The IDF version has an M4-style armored cover for the air intake, and its associated splash guard. This particular example is fabricated from flat plates, as were many of the French-modified M4A4T (*Transforme*), M4A2T and M4A3T Shermans that were retrofitted with Continental R975 radial engines. This is one of several such styles. Given the apparent absence of similar modifications to Priests on display in France, it is highly likely that this change was made in Israel, before they were introduced into service.

The original sponson storage boxes were modified with four handles/tie-downs. The entire engine deck is an adaptation of a standard deck from the Medium Tank M4, and the arrangement of filler caps is different to the standard M7. Note that it has the added oil filler cap on the rear portion, along with two fuel caps on each side of the vent. The latter was a common feature on early M4s (Sherman I) and M4A1s (Sherman II).

This is a rear view of the travel lock and its mount.

Another added feature on IDF Priests was the Sherman-style direct-fire gun sight mounted above the driver station. This was not exactly an accurate device, as it was used only to align the vehicle. Thus, as described in the text, the *KA'AT* aimed the weapon down the barrel in order to destroy that T-34/85. Note how the howitzer was mounted asymmetrically.

This is an overall view of the left interior. The early-production M7s had riveted lower hulls, resulting in the howitzer trail being incorporated in a like manner. Note the folding crew seats flanking the left trail with one which swivels, attached to the mount.

This is a close-up view of the mounting for the communications equipment.

In this view of the left-side of the howitzer, note the recoil spring underneath and the gear teeth for the traverse mechanism.

The deck with its folding access hatches that covers the drive shaft and additional ammunition stowage.

In this general view of the right interior, note the recoil slide and the machine gun mount in the pulpit. The clip on the outside of the pulpit was not a standard American fitting. In the absence of a base for a rifle butt, this may be for a spare .50 caliber barrel.

Close-up view of the right-side of the howitzer.

Ammunition was stored in fiber tubes placed in the bins. In the early versions, the tops of these tubes were exposed, above the side armor.

The rear folding retrofitted armor plate is missing on the IDF vehicles. This is a clear view of the armored vent cover and the cable reel on the right in the photograph, along with the post used to secure the hinged side panel. There is also an added clip for a rifle, toward the top edge of the firewall.

This is a closer view of the mount for the cable reel. Note the connection for the telephone cable. (Joshua Weingarten)

This is one of 20 Priests provided to local *HAGMAR* defense forces, following the *Yom Kippur* War. The engines were removed and, at least in this case, an enclosure covered the area. Two of these Priests were placed at each of 10 *kibbutzim* or *moshavim*, one at each end of a permanent defense position. The howitzers would be manned by local residents, usually reservists or retired veterans. (Michael Mass)

This Priest is located at *Kibbutz* Kinneret which is, not coincidentally, west of Lake Kinneret (Biblical Sea of Galilee), just to the north of Degania Alef and Bet, the scene of that first use of the *Napoleonchik* mentioned in Chapter One. This area is not far from the city of Tiberias, and it just happens to be the *kibbutz*, with its companion *moshav*, that was chosen to test the *HAGMAR* concept (see text). Note the vehicle's welded-on serial number, 864181, just above the fender. (Michael Mass)

The enclosure was permanently attached, plus there were poles for an additional weather cover over the open fighting compartment. Note the mix of road wheels and the T74 steel tracks. (Michael Mass)

This rear view clearly shows the vehicle history in American service, prior to being acquired by France, as it was a common practice to use two stars on the rear sponsons on American M7s. The mound to the left is a portion of the earthen rampart, topped by rocks encased in wire. The hills in the distance are on the Jordanian side of the river. (Michael Mass)

The enclosure nearly fills the old engine compartment, and the rear ammunition bins were re-located inside. Also, there is ample room for other storage. Two brackets for fire extinguishers were added to either side of the enclosure doors. Again, the poles for a weather cover are evident. The interior color looks like the green used for the interiors of the M113 series of APCs. (Michael Mass)

To accommodate the enclosure, the firewall was removed and the forward portion of the engine compartment was plated over. The side fuel tanks were also removed, leaving an exposed sponson floor. The inexperienced local defense troops had ample room to maneuver around the howitzer. (Michael Mass)

Several layers of paint again help to determine the vehicle's history. There are two shades of olive drab and several shades of sand gray, including a distinctly lighter yellowish sandy color that was commonly seen on IDF armor during the early 1960s. The various layers indicate American World War II service, post-war French usage, and IDF service during the 1960s and 1970s, with the darker shade on top. The lighter gray is common for Six-Day War era service. In addition to this example, I have had the opportunity to personally view several similarly chipped paint schemes where I could determine which color was on top of which other color. The yellowish sand is very definitely on top of whatever olive drab, or other original color was used, followed by a grayish sand, sometimes just gray, and then a darker sand gray. (Michael Mass)

This is the same Priest a number of years later, in 2016, after it was moved from its previous location to an area farther inside the *kibbutz*. Of course, it is entirely possible that the *kibbutz* was expanded around it, too. This is a nice view of all of the IDF modifications to the front of the vehicle, including the travel lock, revised tool stowage and the Sherman gun sight. This is also a clear view of the T74 tracks, which are often mistakenly identified as the T54E1 type, simply because of the steel chevron cleats. Instead, the primary visual difference here is the lack of the small protrusions in the center of the track plate edges, as seen on the T54E1. The insert shows how the registration number was applied with weld bead, rather than a stamped plate. The gentleman to the right is Michael Mass. (Jan-Willem de Boer)

The paint is much more deteriorated at this stage, but the 'finish' still provides some interesting information. Looking beyond the rust, there is a finish that looks very much like a yellowish sand color, with an apparent olive drab bleeding through in places. That would be the original American finish. These vehicles were acquired from France, but there is no readily visible evidence of the French brownish color which may mean that they came from surplus storage. Note the riveted lower hull. (Jan-Willem de Boer)

This view is especially useful for understanding the interior layout shown in the following photos. It also shows the articulation of the suspension springs. As it sits on an uneven surface, the bogies have reacted to the distribution of the weight in different ways. Note that on the side, just forward of the bottom row of handles, there seems to be a faint representation of the registration number. (Jan-Willem de Boer)

Unlike the earlier frontal-only view of the rear addition, this angled view more clearly shows its construction, including the door hinge and the relationship of the addition to the original stowage bin. (Jan-Willem de Boer)

Referring back to the right-rear view shown earlier, this is how the engine bay was modified for the vehicle's role in the *HAGMAR* program. The original bay floor now has ammunition bins, like those in the fighting compartment. Note the interior attachment nuts on the bolts for the rear suspension bogies. The open areas with the added shelves are where the original sponson fuel tanks were. (Jan-Willem de Boer)

It is entirely possible that these shelves may have been used for makeshift sleeping bunks, but they may also have been just for additional storage. Note that the original engine access doors are still in place, with the illusion that the vehicle's left door is broken. Actually, that area is the effect from the outside daylight and deliberate photo editing to lighten the interior. (Jan-Willem de Boer)

Here we have a clear view of the driver's station and much of the howitzer itself. Note the elevating gears on the right side of the photo and the traversing gears on the left of the weapon. We can also see the added gun sight for those rare occasions when direct fire is needed, or to simply line up the vehicle with any downrange aiming stakes or a general view of the target area. Refer back to the earlier discussion of the *Yom Kippur* War incident involving the T-34/85, where the *KA'AT* actually aimed down the barrel for a more accurate shot. (Jan-Willem de Boer)

This is the left side of the interior which is included for one primary reason, the added armor plate. Note the vertical line on the upper plate. This is interesting simply because it shows that it was built from two pieces of steel. Another point to note are the four bolts between that seam and the curved portion. This is the external hinge with which the original American vehicles were not equipped. The armor was usually, but not always, added during World War II to protect the exposed shells in the bin seen here and on the other side. The hinges were added later, likely by the IDF. (Jan-Willem de Boer)

3 *TOMAT* M50 155mm

Part 1 – Continental-engined TOMAT

The new *TOMAT* M50s are seen here during an Independence Day parade in Be'er Sheva, on April 16, 1964. The first four vehicles in line, just like the prototype, are fitted with slightly modified, round, Sherman-style air cleaners adapted to fit. The ones following behind have a radically different style. (Fritz Cohen, Israeli Government Press Office)

Towed *TOMAT*

As was also discovered by the American and other armies during World War II, it was soon realized that a larger caliber gun, with greater range was needed to support the growing number of armored units. The reliable Sherman was, once again, chosen as the base vehicle.

The weapon chosen was the French *Obusiers de 155mm Mle 1950* (M50) howitzer which was Israel's first long-range field howitzer. Based on a Finnish design, it entered French service in 1950. First acquired by the IDF in 1956, 36 guns were in service by the early 1960s. They were used as towed howitzers extensively in all major wars, until withdrawn from service in 1980. During the War of Attrition, four guns were dug in at the southern-most position, codenamed *Madved* in the Bar Lev Line, from which they fired over the Canal to the Egyptian side. Some were later given to the SLA which used them until its collapse in 2000. As for the mobile version, initial design work was done at the French company *EFAB* (*Etablissement d'Etudes et de Fabrications d'Armement de Bourges*), with a prototype produced in Israel.

The first long-range field piece obtained by Israel was the French *Obusiers de 155mm Mle 1950* (M50). Such newly-acquired weapons and vehicles were often put on display for the general public. This M50 howitzer was part of an exhibition, actually a Defense Fund rally, in Tel Aviv's Mugrabi Square in March, 1956. Nearby, at the lower right in the photo, is one of the newly acquired *AMX*-13 light tanks. (Israeli Government Press Office)

In 1957, an instructor at the Artillery School gives cadets directions as they practice traversing the Model 1950 howitzer. The practical use for the pedestal is made very clear in this image. In the lower left corner is the loading tray for the 155mm shell. (Israeli Government Press Office)

This M50 crew is going through the loading sequence just prior to the Six-Day War in June 1967. They wear French fatigues and both American and British-style helmets. The loaders carry the projectile in a special tray, used to align the round with the breech. (Israeli Government Press Office)

This is a rear view of the same crew. In this photograph, the loaders' tray is resting on the howitzer mount in a way that ensures that the projectile will be rammed in a straight line into the open breech. The scene could be either the central or northern front, facing either the Jordanians or Syrians. Note that the circular pedestal beneath the howitzer is deployed. With this device deployed to its full extent, the weapon is functionally traversable through 360 degrees if needed, and if the position allows for it. (Israeli Government Press Office)

This battery was in action against Jordanian forces in 1967. Note that the wheels, in this case, are off the ground, allowing the crew to turn the howitzer the full 360 degrees if necessary. This differs from the concept used with the 25-pounder where the tires actually rest on the turntable. (Defense Establishment Archives)

The French-style camouflage fatigues identify this photo as being from 1967. This is also either in the Jordan Valley or on the Golan Heights, obviously after the Six-Day War, or during a lull in the fighting. Artillery battalions usually consisted of 12 guns, so the #10 may be this howitzer's place in line. A weight class is out of the question, since the howitzer weighed less than that. (Defense Establishment Archives)

Prior to the War of Attrition (*Milhemet Ha'Hatashah*) and the *Yom Kippur* War, the IDF built a system of fixed positions, collectively known as The Bar Lev Line, consisting of 16 *Ma'ozim* (*Ma'oz* is defined as 'castle keep', the strongest part of a castle's defense) directly on the Canal, and 12 *Ta'ozim* (strongholds) situated in a secondary line, four to six miles to the east. Generally, the positions themselves were equipped with machine guns, light anti-aircraft guns and mortars, except the southern-most position, code-named *Madved*. Some sources also refer to the name as 'Budapest'. It was equipped with four towed M50 155mm howitzers in bomb-proof emplacements. Immediately before the start of the *Yom Kippur* War, two towed 160mm mortars were delivered, but only one may have been emplaced in time. These photos show two of the four M50s. (Defense Establishment Archives)

This design was still being used in Lebanon in the 1980s. The Israelis provided some to the SLA (**S**outh **L**ebanon **A**rmy), with other factions using guns formerly belonging to the regular Lebanese Army. Since this example is displayed with other captured equipment in July 1982, it more likely belonged to one of the SLA's opponents. (Israeli Government Press Office)

The M50 howitzer could effectively reach a distance of just over 11 miles (17.8 kilometers) with a rate of fire of two rounds per minute. This range allowed the four guns at *Madved* to reach Suez City, across the Canal. This gun is displayed at *Beit Ha'Totchan*. Note how the wheels turn inward as the trail is deployed. This is also a nice close-up view of the fully retractable firing pedestal used to stabilize the howitzer and allow for the 360-degree traverse capability in action. (Right: Guri Roth. Below: Joshua Weingarten)

This is the development vehicle for the *TOMAT* M50 155mm howitzer. A standard M4A4 (Sherman V) hull, powered by the Continental R975 radial gasoline engine, was cut down to the sponson floor at the rear, but the forward portion was cut to the level seen here. The cut left a small section of the original co-driver's hood intact. At this stage, the driver's compartment is taking shape, but it is impossible to tell about the engine compartment, to its right. At least something was done by this point because what appears to be a bulkhead is visible through the bow machine gun port. The gun is in place, and the initial temporary framework for the gun compartment sides is there as well. The actual production vehicle was welded together with no internal frame. Note the hull to the right in the photo, which is the prototype for a low-profile M-50 tank. Designated the M-50 *Degem Yod* (J), it was not adopted for service. (Michael Mass)

Radial-Engined *TOMAT*

The photograph above shows the development vehicle in a workshop. The photograph on page 68 shows an incomplete vehicle, apparently in the open. Identified in a 403 Battalion information publication as the first one delivered to that unit, it is very likely the same vehicle as in the photo above, assigned to the battalion for field trials. Indications are that it was, indeed, still in the development stages.

It is common practice in industry to identify work-in-progress inventory, as such, by marking it in some manner in order to differentiate it, as well as other items intended for use with or on it, as it moves through the production process. These markings may be chalked on, painted on, or be removable labels of some kind. This would be especially important in order to keep track of various test objects, and at what stage they were used. For example: American military practice was to label developmental or test vehicles with a 'T' number, with subsequent stages as 'T#E#'. During World War II, for instance, the T26E3 was standardized as the M26 Pershing. Variants within a series would be M#A#, such as M4A4, which was fitted with a different engine from that used in the original standardized version. Additional test subjects may be further appended, as in M4A3E2, which was built in only limited numbers and featured additional armor plate. It carried the E2 suffix, throughout its service.

Following a field trial, the designers may note the relative effectiveness of a particular combination of features, and decide to either accept it for production, or to move on to another option. For instance, the left rear ammunition storage bin, marked with *MIS' 33* (No.33 in Hebrew), was not actually a real bin with a door. It appears to be a simulated bin, extending outward beyond the side panel, possibly to test for a location relative to other features. The side panel itself is marked separately, also with *MIS' 33*, possibly indicating a combination of two features undergoing a test fit together. The side panel also does not have what will ultimately be the characteristic downward slope to the rear, as seen on vehicles in service. Following this marking theory, final features such as the sloping side panel with, or without, its integrated storage bins, may have a higher number(s).

The design and development stage was completed in early 1963, and 120 surplus NATO howitzers were purchased for the new vehicles. The conversions themselves were done at plant *BM*-1 (Acronym *Bet Mem* for Base Workshop 1) at Tel Hashomer (Hebrew for 'Hill of the Guardsman'). Located in central Israel, it is now home to, among other things, the *Merkava* assembly plant, the IDF Ordnance Corps and the main IDF induction center for new draftees.

The new self-propelled howitzer was called *TOMAT* M50 155mm. (Translation provided by an Israeli Artillery Corps veteran.)

TOMAT is a Hebrew acronym for 'self-propelled gun', pronounced as a single word.

T is the Hebrew letter *Taf*, as ***T**otach* = gun.

O stands for the Hebrew letter *Vav*, used here for pronunciation purposes.

MAT comes from the word ***M**i**T**nayea* = self-propelled.

Note the use of 'M50', without a hyphen, since this is how I saw the designation in an Artillery Corp publication. Unlike the other Sherman variants, which are identified by the type of gun, with a hyphen, they appear to simply insert the French designation unaltered.

Production vehicles entered service with 403 Battalion in 1964. By that time, the forward hull was widened to allow ready-round storage in the gun compartment and to accommodate side stowage bins. The sloping side panels were also now very evident in period photographs. The suspension was otherwise unchanged, resulting in a noticeable overhang above the narrow VVSS (**V**ertical **V**olute **S**pring **S**uspension) tracks.

To stabilize the vehicle during firing, large metal wedge-shaped chocking blocks were placed behind the tracks. The troops referred to these as *Sandalim* (sandals). Because of their size and weight, approximately 110 pounds (50 kilograms), they also became a handy disciplinary tool for officers and non-commissioned officers, as occasionally someone was required to carry one of them, while running a short distance, to atone for some infraction. These chocks were carried in racks at the rear of the vehicle, just below the two large ammunition bin doors.

This is the inside of this prototype vehicle, showing the sides being welded on. One of the braces is shown in the corner, while other posts are used to support the side panel as it is welded along the back edge. What is possibly the M-50 *Degem Yod* is visible through the front opening. (Defense Establishment Archives)

The first of these new long-range mobile howitzers appear to be based on the longer M4A4 (Sherman V) hull, with its wider bogie spacing. As with other M4A4-based vehicles in IDF service, before the upgrade to the Cummins diesel they were powered by the Continental R975 radial gasoline engine. Early production vehicles also used the 3-piece bolted FDA (**F**inal **D**rive **A**ssembly), as used on all production M4A4s. To meet quantity requirements, and in the absence of sufficient surplus M4A4s, other conversions were done using standard short-hull Shermans. This required an extensive effort to lengthen them to M4A4 standards. The hulls were cut and stretched by approximately 11 inches (27–28 centimeters), just as with the basic M4A4. Careful examinations of existing display vehicles shows prominent weld seams where the extensions were added. Furthermore, since the bogie locations were changed to evenly spread the vehicle's weight over the entire suspension, the older bolt holes are noticeably filled with weld material. The extension was added toward the rear of the vehicle, with the welds visible on HVSS (**H**orizontal **V**olute **S**pring **S**uspension) vehicles between the rear large return roller and the rear-most bogie mount. In fact, the forward weld seam bisects the second large return roller mount. The location, near the gun, avoided interfering with the front-mounted engine, but it also meant that the bolts for the return roller and the solid construction of the gun mount, internal ammunition bins and so on, all helped to stabilize the inserted area.

The vehicle was quite wide, at 10.67 feet (3.25 meters), compared to 10.33 feet (3.14 meters) feet for the American M40 155mm SP howitzer, with which it shares more than a slight family resemblance. Without the gun, it was 18.96 feet (5.78 meters) long, while the M40 was longer, at 34.4 feet (7.13 meters). The howitzer mount was capable of higher elevation than in the M40, but its range was shorter by 3.6 miles (5.8 kilometers), at approximately 11 miles (17.7 kilometers). However, this was more than adequate for the region, especially across the Canal, during the War of Attrition. The rate of fire, according to Rafi Marom, an Israeli friend and a Sherman driver in the Artillery Corps, was three

This may be the same vehicle as shown in the previous two photographs. In fact, several features point to it being a development vehicle, as opposed to a production version, even one in progress. The box at the rear is a simulated ammunition storage bin, without a door. It extends outward from the side panel. The latter is very plain with no indication of bin doors, plus it sits out level with the tracks. Note also that the air cleaner is near the edge, whereas on the production vehicle it was inset a little. According to the booklet cited below, this is the first vehicle given to that unit in 1963 even though, in the author's opinion, it is not yet complete. All of this lends credence to the idea that it was issued for troop trials, leading to the final layout seen on production vehicles. (*MISHPACHAT TOTCHANEI EYAL*, issued by 403 Battalion. It contains the unit's unofficial history. A copy can be seen at *Beit Ha'Totchan*)

During the same 1964 parade as the chapter-opening photo, number 811557 passes Prime Minister Levi Eshkol in the lighter colored suit. The saluting officer is the IDF Chief of Staff, the late Yitzhak Rabin, and the other officer is *Aluf* (Major General) Zvi Zamir, Officer Commanding, Southern Command. Note the *sandalim*, or recoil wedges, the angled plates stowed at the rear of the vehicles, in this and several later photos. Visual indications are that these early versions were all built on standard M4A4 hulls. At the very least, they all appear to have the 3-piece FDA (Final Drive Assembly). Later, as the need for mobile artillery increased, the conversion process also included standard-length hulls which were stretched, as described in the text. (Fritz Cohen, Israeli Government Press Office)

to four rounds a minute, although he reports that he heard of a crew, in 1973, doing five rounds per minute.

As with the American Sherman-based M12 and M40, the engine was at the front on both early and late production vehicles, thus allowing room for the crew to manually ram ammunition and to provide an area for crew members to maneuver. The major components of the rear portion were also the same on early and late vehicles. As shown on the three existing museum display vehicles, compartments containing the crew seats and some projectile storage, flank the gun. Beneath the side ammunition stowage racks were four storage bins with outside access doors on each side. Other ready-round projectiles were stored in individual tubes, below the gun. Powder bags were stored in tubes in two large rear-opening, handed vertical bins.

As originally designed, the forward portion of the upper hull was cut down to a level just above the lower edge of the drivers' hoods. Sherman gun tanks were manned by a crew of five. One of them was seated to the right of the driver. He is often referred to as the co-driver, even in the absence of any controls, bow machine gun or radio operator. Also, early and mid-production Shermans had a front plate set at 56 degrees back from vertical, with prominent protruding armored 'hoods', for both the driver and co-driver. These hoods were separate pieces welded in place. Their shape and means of construction varied, depending on the model and manufacturer. They were later eliminated with the introduction of a smooth front plate, set at the steeper angle of 47 degrees. A portion of the lower edges of these hoods are visible in some photographs. The ball mount for the bow machine gun was replaced with a ventilator like the one adjacent to the turret, inside the turret race splash-guard on a standard Sherman. A new driver's hatch was added, slightly raised above the deck. The deck area behind the old ball mount was covered by several access hatches, with large hinges along the front edge. Beneath these hatches is another unique feature of these vehicles.

In the original Sherman, the problems caused by the large size of the rear-mounted radial engine and the subsequent length of the drive shaft for the front-mounted transmission, were resolved by building a higher hull. A front-mounted engine, with a downward slope to accommodate its larger size relative to the transmission, resulted in the need for a much shorter

A column of *TOMAT* M50s participates in the Independence Day parade in Tel Aviv, 1965. By this time, additional stowage was evident, including the multi-piece rammer and the *sandalim* on the rear. This is also a good view of the engine deck showing the standard M4-style radial air vent, with a rack for the gun cleaning rods on the top. (Public Domain, Wikimedia Commons, under GNU Free Documentation License)

In another photograph from the same 1965 parade in Tel Aviv, the drivers still wore the brown Czech version of the Soviet World War II tanker's helmet. Interestingly enough, the drivers in some previous photos, dated a year earlier, have the American style tanker's helmet. In all of these parade photos, the sloping side panels are clearly shown. (Fritz Cohen, Israeli Government Press Office)

The *sandalim* are not often seen being used. Taken during a training exercise prior to the Six-Day War, this photo shows crew members loading the howitzer, while a couple of them look at the photographer, obviously confirming the lack of combat urgency. Also, since the 1967 war was fought in the summer, the cold-weather clothing indicates fall or winter as the timeframe. Note the mix of headgear, including both American and British style steel helmets and the Soviet style tanker's helmet, likely worn by the driver. (Israeli Government Press Office)

drive shaft, in a confined space. Consequently, the Israeli engineers constructed a series of linkages that essentially turned the drive shaft back on itself, in crossed sections, to connect with the original transmission and final drive. On these early vehicles, a standard M4-style air vent, with its typical cover and splash-guard, was mounted on the engine deck, over the fan. Also, two large vent tubes were installed beneath the hull, to help draw the required large volume of cooling air from the rear of the vehicle, into the engine compartment. These extend all the way back, and are still visible under the rear of the hull on display vehicles. The hot exhaust exited to the sides from two pipes at the front of the fighting compartment. Large air cleaners, in at least three different styles on different vehicles, were attached above the exhausts. Two smaller flat vents sat in front of the exhausts, and a standard round armored Sherman sponson vent was mounted on the left front sponson, next to the driver position.

Since even well-tuned radial gasoline-driven engines tended to burn oil, when the engine was shut down, this oil tended to accumulate in the lower cylinders, through the segmented portions of the exhaust, and on the floor of the engine compartment. An engine idle, for more than 30 minutes, meant a larger build-up of oil, so care had to be taken when starting up. Fire was a danger, so there was always a crewman standing by with a fire extinguisher when the engine was started. Accumulated oil could also fill the lower cylinders and cause them to lock up. A manual crank, inserted into an angled hole in the deck, was required to turn over the engine, enough to clear the cylinders. This was quite a tedious task, as two full revolutions, requiring thirty-two turns of the crank, were often needed. A friend, an Artillery Corps veteran who served in a *TOMAT* M50-equipped battalion during the War of Attrition, told a story about a crew's attempts to drive a vehicle, with a bad engine, from its firing position to a transporter, on a nearby road. The oil accumulation and heat build-up were so

Compare this photograph, with the one of the prototype. This is a 1964–1967 era *TOMAT* M50, with the photograph taken during an IDF exhibition intended to display new vehicles and weapons,for senior military and government officials. Some of these were closed to the general public, but others were open to allow the people to see the material and to feel a stronger sense of security. This SPH (**S**elf-**p**ropelled **H**owitzer) was converted from a later-production M4A4, with the cast hoods and 3-piece FDA. The added width, to accommodate the side storage bins, is very evident. Lastly, note the small extended protrusions (bumps stops) on the centre-line of the track plates, identifying these as T54E1s. (Defense Establishment Archives)

bad that two crewmen stood on the engine deck, with fire extinguishers to fight the several fires that broke out, before they finally reached the transporter. The Continental was seriously overloaded and this friend also mentioned that, on every mission, there was a need to tow at least one vehicle because of engine failure.

As mentioned, and ignoring objections to the contrary from some who were concerned about ground pressure, the early Continental vehicles were fitted with the VVSS, and saw action as such, during the Six-Day War. The vehicles equipped three battalions, the previously mentioned 403 Battalion and 872 Battalion in the south, with 871 Battalion in the north.

Any self-propelled artillery piece with its weapon in other than a fully traversable turret, has issues with deflection. In this case, the howitzer could traverse up to 16 or 17 degrees to each side. However, the unequal numbers presented a problem, compounded by the fact that, according to sources, the degrees varied from vehicle to vehicle. Any angle of deflection, beyond what was available to a given vehicle, required that the entire vehicle be turned. When done by an entire battery to cover an entirely different target area, this movement is expressed in Hebrew, as *Tzidud* (turning) *Rachav* (large). All gunnery calculations at that time were done manually, without computers or even calculators. This presented a considerable timing challenge to the fire control teams, as there could be multiple targets, per battery.

By 1969, these vehicles were finally fitted with HVSS. Photographs of the upgraded Continental versions also show that the open-top stowage bins, on the right side of the engine deck, were replaced with larger enclosed bins which extended above the engine deck level. Other than these new bins, and the spare tracks being relocated from the glacis to the left side, little else was visibly changed. In this configuration, they were used extensively in action, during the War of Attrition.

As with any IDF upgrades, it is very likely that both VVSS and HVSS models were actively serving at the same time, albeit in different units. It is highly unlikely that such a valuable weapon system would be completely withdrawn and unavailable during a time of conflict, particularly one as intense and artillery-driven as the War of Attrition. An Artillery Corps veteran explained that upgrades would be done on enough vehicles to equip a battalion. When an active unit was pulled from the line for rest, refit and re-training, the new vehicles would be swapped for its older pieces.

Consequently, during this time in use, the different versions were differentiated according to the suspension. This is further validation for both types being in service simultaneously. Thus, the early VVSS vehicle is known as *TOMAT* M50 155mm *MAZKOM Tzar*, and the HVSS vehicle is known as *TOMAT* M50 155mm *MAZKOM Rachav*. (Translation provided by an Israeli Artillery Corps veteran.)

MAZKOM is the acronym for the suspension and tracks, again pronounced as a single word.

M stands for *Mem*, as in ***M**aarechet* = system
A is *Aleph*, for pronunciation only
Z stands for the Hebrew letter *Zayin*, as in ***Z**echalim* = the track
K stands for *Kuf*, as in ***K**fitzim* = springs
O is *Vav*, for pronunciation only.
M, as in ***M**erkavim* = carrier (mechanics)

Also, compare this photograph with the one of the prototype. This is another 1964–1967-era vehicle, with this photograph taken during training. Note the spare narrow track on the front and the different style of air cleaner on the front of the fighting compartment. The vehicle belonged to 402 Battalion. (Michael Boasson, IDF Artillery Corps veteran)

Tzar means 'narrow', for the 16-inch wide VVSS T54E1 or T74 tracks.
Rachav means 'wide', for the 23-inch wide HVSS T80 tracks.

Immediately after the end of open hostilities in June 1967, several fronts developed along which there was occasional fighting. These areas included the border with Lebanon, Bet She'an Valley, below Lake Kinneret (Biblical Sea of Galilee) and just above the newly occupied West Bank (Occupied Territories), the Jordan River Valley and the *Ramat Ha'Golan* (Golan Heights). Much of this activity had to do with rocket attacks, as well as Jordanian artillery fire. The southern front was, however, the most active and most publicized.

Officially, the War of Attrition along the Egyptian front was fought between March of 1969 and August, 1970. However, it could actually be traced back to the so-called end of the Six-Day War. As early as October 24, 1967, in retaliation for the Egyptian sinking of the Israeli destroyer INS Eilat, 402 Battalion sent two batteries to fire on the oil refineries at Suez. The refineries burned for days afterward. Previous to that, in July, the Egyptians had attacked across the Canal at Ras al Ush, south of Port Fuad, reinforcing the fact that the Six-Day War never really ended after all. Fighting continued, despite the 'official' ceasefire, through October, after which there was a five-month period of relative calm along the Canal.

During this time, the IDF prepared a plan for the strategic defense of the Sinai, known as Operation Dovecote (*Shovach Yonim*). Before a series of fixed fortifications, known in Hebrew as *Ma'ozim*, were erected along the Suez Canal, IDF armored units and self-propelled artillery units were positioned a short distance away to the east. Each unit, a battery in the case of self-propelled artillery, was responsible for a long stretch of the Canal. Mobility was important, and the aforementioned problems with the narrow VVSS suspensions were very evident. To avoid Egyptian counter-battery fire, which was prone to covering a wide area, with a number of weapons that were not necessarily accurately aimed, it was a common practice for a battery to fire for a period of time before changing its location in a rapid movement, known in Hebrew, as *Dilug*. In other cases, re-locations were planned to avoid the possibility of an emergency move. In one such planned re-location, a battery of *TOMAT* M50 155mm howitzers moved 12 miles (20 kilometers) to another location along the Canal, from which it resumed firing. Such actions hastened the conversion to HVSS, with its wider tracks and reduced ground pressure.

After nightfall, during a rehearsal the night before the 1966 Independence Day parade in Haifa, this unit drives along *Ha'Haganah* Avenue, next to the beach. The vehicle's registration number, 79044. It has five digits which indicates that it was, at an earlier time, an M4A4 gun tank, subsequently converted to this SPH. It is also shown again later, after the Egyptians captured it, during the *Yom Kippur* War. (Defense Establishment Archives)

The following day, the real parade was staged on the same street, after which it rolled into the city. Note the weight classification on the FDA, which reads '36', unlike those shown earlier and after this photo, which say '34'. (The Israel Sun, via Central Zionist Archives)

The entire system of fixed positions, collectively known as The Bar Lev Line, consisted of the *Ma'ozim*, directly on the Canal, 16 of which were built, and 12 *Ta'ozim* (artillery strongholds) situated in a secondary line four to six miles to the east. Some sources define a *Ma'oz* as Hebrew for 'castle keep' which was considered the strongest part of a medieval castle's defense. Ironically, it was also usually its last line of defense. The entire Bar Lev Line was subjected to regular, and intense, Egyptian artillery and air attacks.

Generally, the positions themselves were equipped with machine guns, light anti-aircraft guns and mortars, except the southern-most position, code-named *Madved*. It was equipped with four towed M50 155mm howitzers, in bomb-proof emplacements. Immediately before the start of the *Yom Kippur* War, two towed 160mm mortars were delivered, but only one may have been emplaced in time. It is unclear, if the mortars were actually used. This position guarded the southern entrance of the Canal, and dominated Suez City.

All other artillery support was provided by self-propelled units which made do with temporary emplacements dug in the sand. The upside to this was the ability for these units to quickly change location, to avoid counter-battery fire. It also provided the opportunity to be where they were needed, when they were needed. To facilitate movement for these units, as well as armored units and mobile infantry, a series of roads was built, including Artillery Road which ran parallel to the Canal. Other roads ran east to west, to link Artillery Road to other IDF positions.

To further illustrate the nature of the more or less continuous conflict between 1967 and 1973, the experiences of 402 Battalion, which received its *TOMAT* M50 155mm howitzers right after the Six-Day War, are described as a series of actions against either the Palestine Liberation Organization (PLO) or in response to direct enemy action. From its base in Jalameh, near Haifa, units were regularly dispatched to fight in the Beit She'an Valley, just south of Lake Kinneret (Biblical Sea of Galilee). In March 1968, in what was called the *Karameh* Operation, the entire battalion was sent to the Jericho area at the other, southern, end of the Jordan River Valley, to respond to Jordanian fire. In a day-long action, using aerial observers, the unit fought against Jordanian 155mm 'Long Toms' and other targets. Afterward, 402 stayed on alert in the area for a few more weeks.

The Six-Day War started on June 5 with a surprise series of air strikes against the Egyptian Air Force. Shortly afterward, IDF armored units attacked in the Sinai. This *TOMAT* M50 is standing by to support that attack. It sits at the base of a rocky cliff, probably in the southern portion of the front. This vehicle has a 34-ton weight classification marking which consists of white numbers on a red disk, with a blue surround. Note also the casting numbers on the outside sections of the bolted FDA, the T74 tracks lacking the cleats on the edges, and the oil cans on the both sides of the glacis. (Israeli Government Press Office)

By the official start of the War of Attrition, the bulk of the artillery missions were being handled by three regular *TOMAT* M50 battalions, 402, 403 and 404. Together, they made up 209 Artillery *EGGED* (Hebrew for a collection of artillery battalions). Normally, two of the battalions were deployed in battery strength along a long line as the third rested, refitted and trained near Bir Gafgafa (renamed Refidim in Hebrew). This was the site of the principal supply and command complex in the Sinai, about 50 miles from the Canal, along the Central Road beyond the Khatmia Pass. Sometimes, the circumstances called for all three units to be in action simultaneously. From time to time, the regular 334 Battalion, equipped with self-propelled 160mm mortars, the reserve 822 Battalion (Priests) and other reserve *TOMAT* M50 units participated, as needed.

With the artillery units spread thinly across a long distance, and the need for constant activity, service in the Sinai during this period was grueling. In addition to conducting regular firing missions, day and night, they had to assist IDF commandos in raids across the Canal, and to defend against similar raids by Egyptian commando teams.

As described earlier, the radial-powered *TOMAT* M50s suffered from a number of problems associated with having what is essentially an aircraft engine in a confined space, compounded by having to operate these vehicles in a harsh desert environment. Given the distances traveled in the Sinai, and the frequency with which this was done, the problems simply got worse. Such problems previously plagued the other Shermans in the Israeli fleet, prompting a program to replace the Continental engine in the gun tanks.

This photo was altered by a staff person at the Defense Establishment Archives or elsewhere, as indicated by the redacted registration number. The crew appears to be waiting to move out, perhaps to head toward a training exercise, or a ceremony of some sort. The timeline is most likely just before the Six-Day War. (Defense Establishment Archives)

The opening theater of operations in the Six-Day War was on the Egyptian front, in the Sinai Desert. This *TOMAT* M50, registration number 811413, is seen there either before or after some combat. The tracks here are also the T74 type, again without the small cleats below the chevron and along the edges. Other notable features include the 'hood' portion at the old co-driver's position, the use of the old bow machine gun port for the ventilator and the air cleaners. Note also the drain holes in the side storage bins,the applique armor in front of the driver, and also the exhaust at the base of the front of the fighting compartment. (Defense Establishment Archives)

This crew is relaxed and in good spirits as this howitzer is returning from action on the Sinai front in 1967. It is, otherwise, a nice close-up of an early *TOMAT* M50. Note the three sets of hinges on the forward edge of the deck for access to the Continental radial engine. Also, this vehicle does not have the vestige of the co-driver's hood, which may mean that it was converted from a tank with the direct-vision feature. The flat portion of the glacis in that case extends a little higher. (David Rubinger, Israeli Government Press Office)

Admittedly, this is a poor-quality photo. However, its inclusion here is to further illustrate the forward deck. The three hatch lids are over the engine which is offset to the vehicle's right. Maintenance of the Continental engine was awkward with any major work, especially beyond an arm's length into the engine bay which required the actual removal of the engine. This full-side view does show the *sandalim* in place, and the commander has covered his ears as the gunner prepares to pull the lanyard. (Original source unknown, but it was scanned from a book, at some point.)

Here is a battery in action on the Golan Heights, June 1967. The crews are relaxed, but standing at the ready awaiting orders to load and fire. The long handles for the rammers are evident, and there is very likely a shell sitting in the loading rack. (Defense Establishment Archives)

The IDF parade in 1968 was also held in Jerusalem in a special commemoration of the city being reunited. In this photograph, a battery of five *TOMAT* M50 155s follows another, as they drive toward the reviewing stand. The Old City, a significant part of Jewish/Israeli history, is somewhere to the right, in the photo. (Fritz Cohen, Israeli Government Press Office)

By 1969, the M50 was being re-fitted with the wide track HVSS suspension, to be designated *TOMAT* M50 155mm *MAZKOM Rachav*. In this photograph, 402 Battalion is in formation, after training near Bir Gafgafa in the Sinai, east of The Great Bitter Lake and Ismailia. In addition to the suspension change, more storage was added in the form of an enclosed bin on the right sponson in front of the gun compartment. It is fitted with two full height doors, opening to the side. (Photographed by a member of 402 Battalion, via Itamar Rotlevi)

This photograph shows five howitzers, five half-tracks, three of which have raised sun screens, so they are likely to be *MAPIKS*, and two M601 Dodge Power Wagons. The latter was a military version of the Dodge Power Wagon pickup truck which was built for American civilian use after World War II. These successors to the WC series ¾-ton Weapons Carrier were also assembled in Israel under license from the Chrysler Corporation. They were extensively used by the IDF. (Photographed by a member of 402 Battalion, via Itamar Rotlevi)

It should be noted that the various upgrades and revisions to IDF armored vehicles were done intermittently, not all at once, when the various units were withdrawn from front-line positions or other active duty. This was particularly true for the TOMAT M50s being retrofitted with HVSS and, later, the Cummins engine.402 Battalion, for instance, was in action during the initial stages of the War of Attrition as built, including the VVSS (**V**ertical **V**olute **S**uspension **S**ystem). At one point, their vehicles were swapped out, and the older ones were sent for the refit. This technician is in the process of this. Typically, vehicles were stripped down and re-built, and he is adjusting the storage bin before the spare tracks are added. Note the suspension bogie unit, which has a mid-production skid on top. (Defense Establishment Archives)

One of the 402's vehicles is seen here during preparations for an exercise. Note that the howitzer barrel is free of the travel lock, and the gun commander is on the field telephone, likely speaking with the fire control team. The new storage bin is visible on the right side, and the suspension has dramatically changed the vehicle's overall appearance. (Photographed by a member of 402 Battalion, via Itamar Rotlevi)

This howitzer crew is preparing to load the shell into the breech, using the loading tray. This will be rammed in far enough to accommodate the number of powder bags required for the distance to be covered. These bags were stored in the two rear lockers, flanking the crew area. The ready-rounds were stowed in front of the lockers, along the sides. (Defense Establishment Archives)

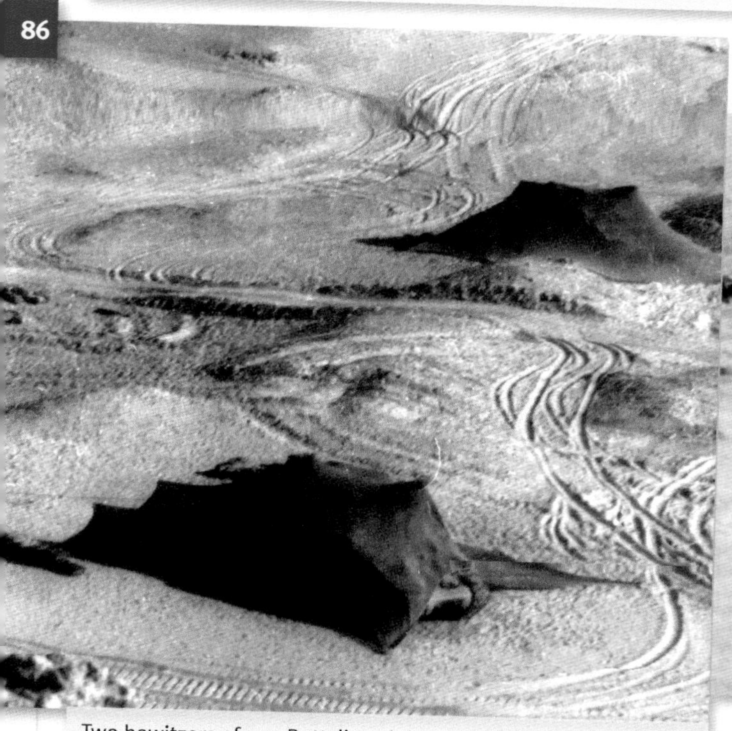

Two howitzers of 402 Battalion sit beneath camouflage netting, somewhere in the area near Ein Musa (Spring of Moses), south of the Canal. Ein Musa is the site of one of the *Ma'ozim*, code name *Mavded* (see text). (Photographed by a member of 402 Battalion, via Itamar Rotlevi)

Later in the year, the 402 was in action along the Canal, opposite Ismailia. The desolate nature of the desert is obvious. Note the staging of the guns. Note also the new storage bin on the right side. One of the half-tracks is the *MAPIK*, described later, housing the fire-control team. (Photographed by a member of 402 Battalion, via Itamar Rotlevi)

Here we see two other guns from 402, with a fire-control team *MAPIK*. In this photograph, a Dornier Do.28 patrol and reconnaissance plane (known as *Dror* in Israeli service – Sparrow in English), likely carrying an aerial observer, is doing a low-level fly-by. Note the crewman waving at the plane. (Photographed by a member of 402 Battalion, via Itamar Rotlevi)

Here is an example of the revised and upgraded *TOMAT* M50 155mm *MAZKOM Rachav*, as of the War of Attrition. The travel lock is released and, otherwise, the gun is ready for action. The crew is going about the business at hand at this moment, to suggest that action is not imminent. Note the stowed camouflage netting and barbed wire. The location is still opposite Ismailia. Air attack was always a threat, so the .50 caliber machine gun is uncovered and ready for use. (Photographed by a member of 402 Battalion, via Itamar Rotlevi)

These two *TOMAT* M50s are caught at the moment of firing. Note the rammer on the ground, and a number of unexpended rounds on the floor, right under the recoiling howitzer in the first photo. There are no empty shells on the ground so, if this is full combat, it has just begun. On the other hand, the second photo indicates, by the large number of expended shells, a period of extended firing, during the War of Attrition. By the start of the *Yom Kippur* War, all Israeli Sherman variants in service had been upgraded with the Cummins diesel engine. Even though most of the front portion of the vehicle is obscured by smoke, the low-profile of the visible part, and the spare track racks, indicate that this is still a Continental version. (Photographed by a member of 402 Battalion, via Itamar Rotlevi & Defense Establishment Archives)

This crew is uncovering its gun in preparation for a firing mission. They wear a mix of headgear, including the British M1943 helmet and the American tanker's helmet. This is a nice close-up shot of several features on this intermediate version. These include the armored vent, just visible behind the driver's hatch lid, and the spare road wheel and track. Note that someone has plugged one of the drain holes, with a rag. (Israeli Government Press Office)

These next three photographs show, in detail, parts of the firing process. The first image shows the gun layer using the wheels to elevate and traverse the howitzer, according to instructions from the aimer, shown here speaking on the field telephone with the fire control team. The 'U'-shaped extension below the breech is to support the rack used to load the projectile. The stamping on the breech identifies the gun as 'OB.155.50 N=655 ATS.1955'. (Israeli Government Press Office)

The direct-fire telescopic sight is shown next to the breech. Note the gun commander at the front, as he is busily looking down at what is likely a gunnery table or map, sitting on a specialized rack, shown in more detail in later photographs. The aimer is looking through the gun sight to the left of the direct-fire sight, as he continues to speak on the field phone. (Israeli Government Press Office)

This offers details of the breech and the way it is threaded. Note the 155mm shell in the background. (Israeli Government Press Office)

This is the same vehicle as in the four previous photographs. At this point the driver, the same soldier previously seen removing the net, is in his seat perhaps ready to move quickly in the event of counter-battery fire from the Egyptians. As described by an Israeli friend who was a driver in the *TOMAT* M50, as well as the *MACHMAT* 160mm, he, when not driving, had varied duties such as being responsible for checking the battery, cleaning the ignition points and checking the fluids. He also cleaned the large air cleaners. Since the machine gun is covered, either there is no immediate threat of air attack, or they are preparing for a routine move. Note the sight vane in front of the driver. This was used to roughly line up the vehicle with a series of aiming sticks planted at intervals, in front of the guns. (Israeli Government Press Office)

In 1970, as the War of Attrition continued, 402 Battalion was once again in action. This time it was in the area east of the Canal, near the city of Kantara, about 31 miles (50 kilometers) south of Port Said. This howitzer is participating in a firing mission. Note the 155mm shell resting on the loading rack, on the floor. (Photographed by a member of 402 Battalion, via Itamar Rotlevi)

The next four photographs illustrate the firing sequence. It took a total of eight men to load and fire the howitzer. This included the driver. In this first image, two crewmen have raised the shell to rest on the rear portion of the breech, while another is ready with the rammer. Note that the rear doors were painted white. (Photographed by a member of 402 Battalion, via Itamar Rotlevi)

It takes the efforts of three men to ram the shell. The soldier on the right must be reacting to a nearby howitzer firing, because this one is not yet ready. Note the nearby tubes containing powder charge bags. The actual charge used depended on the distance,to the target. Options included one large bag and up to four smaller bags. (Photographed by a member of 402 Battalion, via Itamar Rotlevi)

The rammers are moving away as the gunner moves forward to attach the firing lanyard. (Photographed by a member of 402 Battalion, via Itamar Rotlevi)

The lanyard is attached, and the gunner awaits the order to fire. The next shell is already in place for the next re-load sequence. Note the other shells on the floor. (Photographed by a member of 402 Battalion, via Itamar Rotlevi)

Fighting during the War of Attrition went on around the clock, as witnessed by this crew firing in the dark. The downside of this is the muzzle flash, revealing the battery's position, so they had to move often. Referring back to the main text, this was not always accomplished smoothly with the Continental-powered M50s. Battalions were also rotated on a regular basis so, given the lack of white paint on the locker doors, this is likely not 402 Battalion. (Sourced via the Internet, given the age of photo, it is in the Public Domain)

402 Battalion eventually moved back to Bir Gafgafa for rest and training, where it is seen here in 1970, still powered by the Continental radial. (Photographed by a member of 402 Battalion, via Itamar Rotlevi)

4 TOMAT M50 155mm

Part 2 – Cummins-engined TOMAT

The howitzer has just fired and its crew is preparing to move out. The driver is running to his station, and the gunner is removing the lanyard. Following the firing exercise, the vehicles will pass in review. Note that the downward slope of the side panel is very clear as is, once again, the new enlarged profile for the Cummins diesel conversion. Note also, that the *sandalim* are no longer used. (Moshe Milner, Israeli Government Press Office)

Cummins-Engined *TOMAT*

Even before the first Continental-powered *TOMAT* M50 entered production, the IDF had already begun replacing the radial engine in its primary gun tanks, the M-50 and M-51. As this process alone was lengthy and expensive, the *TOMAT* M50 program had to wait until the tank conversions were complete, and beyond. It was not until sometime in 1969 that the conversions began with some regular Artillery Corps units.

By 1973, however, the transition from the older Continental petrol engines to the Cummins diesel (Model VT80-460) was, indeed, complete for all units, resulting in a dramatic change in appearance. To differentiate the upgraded vehicles, they are identified in a book in the library at *Beit Ha'Totchan*, as M2. The front portion of the hull was noticeably higher, with a set of very prominent louvres at the right front of the hull in place of the smaller ventilator. A series of access hatches, some with louvres and some without, covered the rest of the engine deck. The gun compartment remained essentially unchanged internally, but the large air cleaners on the front became unnecessary. The left side open-top bins, and the extended enclosed bins on the right side already mentioned, were replaced by new bins incorporated into the raised forward portion of the vehicle. A large exhaust pipe protruded from an angled inset on the right side.

The Cummins itself was installed offset to the right, requiring another adjustment to accommodate the central drive shaft. The drive shaft solution, in this case, involved a series of short shafts and universal joints that connected to the transmission. The *sandalim* were also no longer needed.

Besides its enhanced reliability, the new engine also increased the speed of the vehicle, somewhat.

In its Cummins configuration, the *TOMAT* M50 weighed 34 tons. The 460-horsepower diesel provided for 2,600 rpm, which, with its 199.4-gallon (755 liters) fuel capacity, allowed for a range of 248.5 miles (400 kilometers).

During the *Yom Kippur* War, these upgraded howitzers saw action on both fronts. Unfortunately, several were captured and put on display in Egypt. After 1973, they were gradually withdrawn from service and replaced by the more modern M107, M110 and M109 types from the United States. However, at the start of the 1982 Operation Peace for Galilee, the IDF still listed, as active, eight *TOMAT* M50 battalions, totaling 96 guns. As of 1997, some were being offered for sale, complete with ammunition, on the Internet. There is no evidence at this time, however, that any *TOMAT* M50 155mm howitzers were actually acquired, and used, by anyone else.

This howitzer was part of a unit participating in a demonstration during the graduation ceremony for a new group of artillery officers, April 1972. The crew is awaiting the order to fire, as the gun commander raises a flag to signal 'Ready'. From this angle, some of the more obvious changes corresponding to the Cummins upgrade can be seen. First, the increased height of the forward upper hull is obvious, as is the auxiliary engine exhaust. The spare-track rack is now mounted above the bins on the rear half of the vehicle. (Moshe Milner, Israeli Government Press Office)

With the firing demonstration completed, the battalion prepares to roll past the officials and generals on the reviewing stand. Because this was purely an exhibition and ceremonial salute, these vehicles were not completely fitted with all of the various tools and such. (Moshe Milner, Israeli Government Press Office)

During the summer of 1973, the crew of this *TOMAT* M50 is seen busy cleaning up the vehicle after an exercise. It is not often that one can see a military vehicle being sprayed with a water hose to get rid of all of the dirt. Apparently, the guy on the right did not want to get his uniform wet, so he's opted to wear, hopefully, a swimsuit and not just his boxers. (Defense Establishment Archives)

This nice full-profile look at the right side of the upgraded vehicle shows the exterior modifications to good effect. The forward side storage bins appear to be a holdover from the previous upgrade of the Continental-powered vehicles to HVSS. Note the engine exhaust, which is explained in more detail later. (Defense Establishment Archives)

These crewmen pose for this photo, obviously during a lull in whatever exercise, or potential combat scenario, is at hand. The markings were, apparently, applied in haste, and the elements were not kind. Note the aiming stakes which are not deployed, further supporting the idea of a lull in activity. They are painted red and white, although I have seen evidence of other colors, such as blue and red, also in use. The guy on the right has appeared in other photos or, at least, he bears a striking resemblance to an instructor in a heavy mortar unit(s). (Defense Establishment Archives)

General Israel Tal commanded the Southern Front, during the *Yom Kippur* War. Here, he is visiting an artillery unit somewhere in the desert. Note the winter weather attire, unlike the rolled-up sleeves in the previous photo, because it does get cold in the desert! Photographic evidence suggests that, when these vehicles went through the refit for the Cummins, even just the HVSS, they also received the cast Final Drive Assembly. (Defense Establishment Archives)

The re-built *TOMAT* M50 155mm *MAZKOM Rachav* with its new engine was soon in combat. The redesign of the forward hull was extensive, dramatically changing the vehicles' appearance. This howitzer was emplaced on the Golan Heights, early in the *Yom Kippur* War. The topography on the *Ramat Ha'Golan* varies from a barren landscape like this, to snow-capped mountains, farms and wooded areas. (Defense Establishment Archives)

In the mad rush to get reinforcements to the front, at least two *TOMAT* M50s were caught up in this jam of vehicles, also on the Golan Heights, on October 13. Also visible are half-tracks, automobiles, a *Sho't* MBT (Centurion) and one of the new M548 cargo carrier variants of the M113 series, known in IDF parlance, as the 'Alpha'. (Ze'ev Spector, Israeli Government Press Office)

There are howitzers from two batteries, dispersed over the rocky terrain of the Golan Heights. The *MAPIK* is in the upper left corner of the photograph. Note that the re-supply vehicles are American GMC 2½-ton trucks, with the one in the background having a soft top. Although the howitzers themselves seem to be devoid of any tactical markings, the truck in the foreground has the black and white air recognition stripe on the hood (bonnet). (Defense Establishment Archives)

There are several points of interest in this photograph, also on the Golan. The most obvious point is that the unit has been involved in heavy firing for some time, given the large pile of empty ammunition containers, each of which held two powder bags. The re-supply truck is a semi-trailer, so access by road was, apparently anyway, available. The crew wears a mix of headgear, including a left-over British 'Brodie', as seen in use back to the War of Independence. The latter was common in reserve units in 1967 and obviously, in 1973. As in the War of Attrition, the rear doors were painted white inside. (Defense Establishment Archives)

This is a closer shot of the same howitzer, firing yet another round. Note the dust on the ground, thrown up by the force of the recoil. Also, the white doors are more obvious here. Shells appear to be thrown around haphazardly, and one in the foreground,is missing a fuse, while a couple more still have the metal handle. Fuses were carried in a separate wooden box. (Defense Establishment Archives)

Here we have another vehicle from the same unit. It appears as though the ammunition pallets were unloaded in a rush. One pallet is upside-down, while the next one has split apart entirely. Note the method of securing the shells. The prime mover is an American-built civilian R-Series Mack tractor unit, quite common in official IDF use. It was also prominent among civilian vehicles commandeered by the military, for use in a state of emergency. The officer, without the helmet and flak vest, is possibly with the supply unit. (Defense Establishment Archives)

Another unit is being re-stocked with ammunition, which, along with the scattered empty cases, indicates an expected sustained rate of fire. Note the drop-sides on the semi-trailer that also carries both shells and powder. The following three photographs show this particular *TOMAT* M50 in various stages of activity. (Defense Establishment Archives)

Ramming the shell is almost done, and another crewman looks as though he is preparing the firing lanyard. (Defense Establishment Archives)

Caught at the moment of firing, the concussion and recoil throw up a lot of dust. Note that many of the crewmen in this series of photographs are wearing American-style Vietnam-era flak jackets. (Defense Establishment Archives)

Once again, the crew is caught at the moment of firing, with the howitzer in full recoil. Note that the next round is already in its loading tray, a necessary step in order to maintain a high rate of fire. Given the amount of detritus around the position, the battery has not yet come under Syrian counter-battery fire, which would force them to move. (Defense Establishment Archives)

Switching to the Egyptian front in 1973, the terrain is much more open. In this photograph, in an area known as *Tzir Akavish* (Spider Route) near the Canal, *BM-24* rocket launchers from 270 Battalion have begun to fire. The *TOMAT* M50s, in the foreground, belong to 834 Battalion. In this case, there are tactical markings visible on one howitzer. The barrage is in support of Sharon's crossing to the western side of the Canal. (Defense Establishment Archives)

Note the sandy terrain in the background of this photograph. This *TOMAT* M50 crew is ramming home a round on the Egyptian front. Points of interest include the loading rack which rests on supports behind the breech, the ammunition storage tubes beneath the howitzer, and the ready-rounds on the floor. The angular shapes on the floor at each side house the idler axle. (Defense Establishment Archives)

The crews of these howitzers are at ease during a break in the action. The crew of the foreground vehicle has placed a ground-mount .30 caliber machine gun on the engine deck. Apparently, there was a danger from roaming groups of Egyptian infantrymen, indicating that the battery is close to the front. (Defense Establishment Archives)

There is a .30 caliber mounted on this vehicle as well, so there may have been a general departure from the .50-caliber. The rear doors on this vehicle are not white, so it may be from a different unit. Note the crewman to the left, with the firing lanyard. (Defense Establishment Archives)

This crew looks as though they have been in action for some time. Fatigue can give way to a certain level of sloppiness in dress. The howitzer was just fired, with the barrel in partial recoil, and the men are protecting their ears from the concussion and noise. Note the white doors again, although this is not a universal feature of the *TOMAT* M50s in this section. Note also, the open ammunition lockers, the ready rounds, and again, a .30 caliber machine gun. (Defense Establishment Archives)

Fighting during the *Yom Kippur* War was, again, around the clock at times. The bright flash gives an almost surreal quality to the terrain. Note the number of shells nearby, indicating both a long fight ahead and a relatively static position. (Defense Establishment Archives)

In this view from the left side of the same howitzer, the vastness of the desert is very evident, even in the dark. Other howitzers are barely visible in the distance. As seen before in one of the photographs on the Golan, the next round is already in the loading tray. It almost looks as though the crew has settled into a routine, without an immediate sense of urgency. They are prepared nonetheless. (Defense Establishment Archives)

This vehicle is approaching a *Magach* (M48 Patton series) MBT (**M**ain **B**attle **T**ank) which places the location on the Egyptian front. American Patton series tanks were used exclusively on the Sinai front in this conflict, given the nature of the terrain. (Defense Establishment Archives)

The next six photographs show various *TOMAT* M50s, on the move on the Golan Heights. The power lines indicate a populated area, although the column is moving cross-country, rather than on the nearby road. They may be moving toward a new firing position, or to a bivouac area. Identification numbers are assigned to the howitzer (on the recuperator), as well as the vehicle (barely visible on the side), just as tank turrets have a separate number. (Defense Establishment Archives)

This vehicle is either on a road or very close to one, given the road sign. Traffic in the Middle East travels on the right side of the road, placing the signage on that side as well. Note the drain holes at the bottom of the side bins. Also, note the number on the howitzer which is not the same as the vehicle's registration. (Defense Establishment Archives)

This *TOMAT* M50 of a reserve battalion is traveling past an idol *Sho't Kal* (IDF-upgraded Centurion) on a road near Bugata on the Golan Heights, on October 8, 1973. Note that the waving soldier is carrying the indigenous version of the Belgian-designed 7.62mm *FN-FAL* rifle. (Defense Establishment Archives)

For an unimportant reason, I find it interesting to see vehicles from wartime photographs, as they are today. Number 810160 is also shown in the color section, at least in a close-up of the transmission cover, as it sits in a relatively present-day storage yard. Here it is on a road on the Golan Heights in 1973, with some of the battalion's support vehicles trailing behind it. (Defense Establishment Archives)

Number 811482 is also from the same unit and the same sequence of photographs. Note that there is no stenciling on the side bins, as seen later in the color section. In fact, none of the photographs to this point show this. No machine gun is mounted and the crew seems a little at ease at this point. Note that the machine guns on all of these vehicles are.30 caliber Brownings. (Defense Establishment Archives)

Here is a third vehicle from the same unit. The serial numbers for these three howitzers are fairly close sequentially, for whatever that is worth. Note the individual vehicle numbers, 6, 10 and 13. Although a typical battalion consisted of 12 tubes, it was not unheard of to have more. The small marking to the right of the white 13, will be in red. (Defense Establishment Archives)

In contrast, these artillerymen are exhausted from the fighting. Several of them are clutching *Uzi*s. Note the empty ready racks, and the rear doors which are, in this case, white. To avoid counter-battery fire from the numerically superior Syrian artillery, these crews would move as many as a dozen or more times during a single day of fighting. (Defense Establishment Archives)

This is an excellent character study of the effects of prolonged fighting on a soldier. Of interest is the carrying rack for the projectile, partially visible behind him, which would rest on the 'U'-shaped bracket under the breech during loading. The man's *FN-FAL* rifle rests next to him. The Belgian-designed *FN-FAL* and the Israeli-designed *Uzi* were both considered by the troops to be inferior to the Soviet-made *AK-47*. The latter was a simple and rugged design created by a Soviet T-34 driver-mechanic, Mikhail Kalashnikov, during World War II. I met this man some years ago at a military vehicle exhibition in Virginia. (Defense Establishment Archives)

Amidst the detritus of combat, this crew finds time and the spirit, to smile for the camera. However, they are obviously still ready to resume firing at a moment's notice. A large number of shells is piled under the howitzer with, in a common theme in these 1973 photographs, a round resting in the loading rack. By the terrain, this scene is on the Egyptian front. (Defense Establishment Archives)

This is definitely during a prolonged lull in the fighting in the Sinai. The rammer has been disassembled and re-stowed on the left side. Other than the neatly arranged and stacked ammunition, there is no indication of recent or impending action. With the howitzer partly covered, the unit may be preparing to move. Of course, with the Fitter half-track sitting there, it may also be a mechanical issue, and rest of the battery has already gone to the next location. (Defense Establishment Archives)

During another break in the fighting, crews perform routine maintenance while also re-stocking food and other supplies. It is also possible that they may be preparing to move to another location along the Canal. The vehicle, only partially visible on the right, is an American-built M113 *Zelda* variant. (Defense Establishment Archives)

This photo was in the same relative sequence as the previous one, so they may have indeed, prepared for a move, perhaps a *Tzidud Rachav*. Just as in the War of Attrition, units were regularly on the move to either escape Egyptian counter-battery fire or simply to support a different armored or infantry action. (Defense Establishment Archives)

Obviously, not all vehicle damage came as a result of combat. Indeed, this may be one of those "Lucy, you haf a lot of 'splainin' to do!" moments, as spoken by Ricky Ricardo (reference made to the 1950s era TV show 'I love Lucy'. Younger readers will have to look that up!). These soldiers, however, do not seem to be concerned about a reprimand, except for the sullen guy not joking around, as two of them pretend to try pulling the vehicle upright. This could be as simple as the transporter hitting a bomb crater or sliding on loose sand. Either way, there will likely be the need for some repairs to the suspension. (Defense Establishment Archives)

Photographs of the Cummins engine itself are rare. Here are the new (right, on its pallet) and the old (left behind the wrecker crewman), during an engine change-out in the field. A large section of the engine deck was removed to do this. The truck's American designation is M816 Truck, Wrecker, Medium, 5-ton 6x6, but the boom, however, bears a plaque from Eyal Industries, so this may be a license-built crane on an M809 series truck. While the maintenance team swaps the engines, the gun crew rests in the shade. (Defense Establishment Archives)

Partially obscured by the new engine, the ID number begins with '109xxx' indicating the vehicle was converted from a captured Egyptian Sherman. (Defense Establishment Archives)

This isolated view of the replacement engine offers a comparison with photographs of the later top-mounted exhaust versions in M-50 and M-51 tanks. The exhaust pipe exits from the same port on the top of the engine, but it angles down to the vehicle's left rear on gun tanks, where it would meet the lower external M4A3-style pipe. In this version, where the engine is mounted in reverse, the same exhaust pipe will exit to the vehicle's right. (Defense Establishment Archives)

This is the same scene from a different perspective. There is a full rear view of the crane truck, plus a decent view of an M32A1B1 ARV (**A**rmored **R**ecovery **V**ehicle) on a cast hull, as it also undergoes an engine change. (Defense Establishment Archives)

The IDF pulled back from the western side of the Canal in February 1974. This crew is very happy to be going home, as they prepare to cross the Canal over the causeway near Deversoir, built to replace one of the pontoon bridges used in the counter-attack. The sign says 'Homeward with great joy'. (Ya'acov Sa'ar, Israeli Government Press Office)

The vehicle next in line also carries a sign with Hebrew writing expressing thoughts from when the Jews first withdrew from Egypt, with a Biblical verse: "and God brought us out from there, with a strong hand and outstretched arm". The phrase 'so long, Africa', being in English could be for the benefit of 'Henry', whose name in Hebrew is within the parentheses on the corrugated sheet at the beginning. Note that this conversion was also done on a captured Egyptian Sherman, with a registration number 109xx8. (Ya'acov Sa'ar, Israeli Government Press Office)

Contrary to some popular beliefs, deserts are not always completely barren of vegetation. Portions of the Negev Desert are actually used for farming and, as shown here, the Sinai has some grass, even if just weeds and trees, as one gets closer to the Canal. This after-action photo shows vehicles of 872 Battalion at rest, somewhere in the Sinai. (872 Battalion Unit History)

Even as the IDF was ultimately successful, a lot of firefights did not end in Israel's favor, obviously. This was especially true during, and immediately after, the initial Egyptian surprise attack across the Canal. From the beginning of the War of Attrition, as shown earlier, artillery units were emplaced along and just behind the Bar-Lev Line. This emplacement, with its *TOMAT* M50 intact, was overrun along with another in the distance. (Unknown Source, via the Internet)

Israel was, indeed, ultimately militarily successful in the *Yom Kippur* War, but there was a cost. Most tragic was the loss of 2,687 soldiers killed, 7,251 wounded and 314 POWs. Equipment was captured as well, such as this *TOMAT* M-50 155mm *MAZKOM Rachav*, registration number 79044. To reduce the negative effect on Egyptian morale, military and civilian, they put this material on display in Ismailia and other places, as though they were victorious. Compare this view with the same vehicle in the 1966 parade in Haifa.

This is the rear view of 79044. Note that the propaganda value of these exhibits was 'enhanced', so to speak, by the inclusion of, for effect, other gear that was no longer in use by Israel, such as the QF 25-pounder to the left. Compare the area below the left side locker door with the earlier photo, of the construction of one of these vehicles. Other features are discussed in detail later.

Some *TOMAT* M50s were simply destroyed, as can be seen here. This vehicle was likely struck by Egyptian artillery fire, but it could also have been hit by tank rounds during a counterattack.

After the *Yom Kippur* War, there was cause for some celebration since Israeli forces had successfully responded to the surprise attacks from two directions. However, there were no more regular IDF parades on Independence Day. However, that did not mean that the public was not treated to a drive-by of troops and equipment for other reasons. Also, there were parades and so on after training or graduation from various schools. This *TOMAT* M50 155mm *MAZKOM Rachav* passes the reviewing stand in one such parade. (Israeli Government Press Office)

Eventually, the half-track *MAPIK* gave way to a more modern vehicle, the American-built M577 command and communications version of the M113 series. One of these is seen here in front of two *TOMAT* M50s, in the same parade as shown in the previous photo.

As mentioned earlier, there are sections of Israel that qualify as desert. A lot of the country, about the size of the state of New Jersey in the US, is lush farmland, forests, and so on. Yes, it does snow in the high country and on the *Ramat Ha'Golan*. Here, we see a battery of *TOMAT* M50s on a winter exercise on the Golan. Although the photo is not dated, it is most likely to be during the mid-to-late 1970s. (Defense Establishment Archives)

After these weapons were retired from service, and after an extended time in storage, in case of a military emergency, the M50s were transported to the recycling plant at Yehuda Steel, to be scrapped. This photo has some interesting points, such as the wooded terrain and the colors of the vehicles. Although the markings indicate this to be a civilian semi-tractor, it was also common for similar IDF vehicles and the cabs of non-combat supply trucks to be painted white. All IDF tank transport trailers are painted yellow, but this one has a civilian license plate. However, it would very likely be 'drafted' into military service in case of war. Lastly, the color of the *TOMAT* M50 is most interesting, especially given the extensive discussions in forums and the amount of disinformation or lack of definitive information from some sources. Basically, this is the color applicable to the 1970s and beyond. Keep in mind that there are variations, due to weathering, touch-ups, repairs and, even the thinner used. (Michael Mass)

There are three *TOMAT* M50 155mm *MAZKOM Rachav* howitzers on display in Israeli museums. This photo was taken in 2005 at *Yad La'Shiryon* (Latrun). The others are at *Beit Ha'Totchan*, in the very nice northern town of Zichron Ya'akov, and at *Batey Haosef* in Tel Aviv-Yafo (Jaffa).

Yad La'Shiryon, 2008: This is based on an M4A4 (Sherman V), so it did not require any lengthening. The most obvious way to identify an original M4A4, from any distance, is the lower rear hull plate which, unlike other Shermans, was vertical. However, that particular identifying feature is missing on the *TOMAT* M50, but the idler mount is there which was also vertically mounted, as seen here. (Guri Roth)

Beit Ha'Totchan, 2005: In contrast to the Latrun example, this vehicle was converted from a short-hull Sherman. This particular hull is an early version that was assembled with rivets which can be clearly seen here. Also, the idler mount is tilted backward to correspond with the original plate, which was angled at the rear. A close look at the area just forward of the rear bogie, and below the large return roller, will show the location of the insert used to lengthen the hull. The missing lower hull rivets are the giveaway.

Beit Ha'Totchan, 2008: In this close-up view, the welds are very clear. The front weld bisects the rear return roller mount. The rear weld is faintly visible, behind the bogie. (Mark Hazzard)

Beit Ha'Totchan: Because the suspension mounts were moved to allow for the increased hull length, the original bolt holes were filled with weld material. Basically, the insert was placed at the rear to allow for its inclusion with the base of the howitzer, for added strength. (Mark Hazzard)

The following photographs, from different years and of several vehicles, provide a detailed all around look at the hull. The photographs in this section provide the proper detail required for an accurate look at the *TOMAT* M50 155mm *MAZKOM Rachav* with the Cummins engine. This is the left side of the front deck on the Latrun vehicle. Note the Hebrew letter, *dalet*, on the filler cap. This is the first letter of *delek*, which means 'fuel'. The front cap has the letter *mem*, which designates water storage.

Yad La'Shiryon, 1992: This earlier photograph shows a fitting which also appears on the vehicle at *Beit Ha'Totchan*. However, there is no provision for it on the vehicle at *Batey Haosef*. It is hinged to fold over the top, where it sits today, in its ready-to-use position, on both vehicles. Note the bracket used to secure it on the outside. With its close proximity to the radio when folded into its normal position inside, it serves as a table, of sorts, for the gun commander with a hinged storage compartment for gunnery charts and maps.

Beit Ha'Totchan, 2005: Note the number '129', made from welding wire, the purpose of which is not confirmed,. This also appears in the rear gun compartment. I presume, however, that it is a production number, assigned during the conversion process. Note that the cap to the left, in the photo, is flat, possibly meaning that it is not armored.

Yad La'Shiryon, 2005: The Latrun vehicle has what appears to be a welded '6' with a line beneath it, albeit in a different location, to differentiate it from '9'. The vehicle at *Batey Haosef* does not have such a similar visible number at all. Note that although the older Continental engine installation suffered from inadequate engine deck ventilation, there was ample provision for cooling air on the Cummins deck.

Beit Ha'Totchan, 2005: The Cummins diesel was installed to the right side, with the radiator and fans toward the front. These louvres are directly above the cooling fans, with the radiator immediately in front of them.

Beit Ha'Totchan, 2005: This photograph completes the views of the closed engine deck. The engine was located beneath these hatches, with the exhaust exiting to the side, just forward of the side storage bins.

In 1992, the vehicle at *Yad La'Shiryon* was fresh from storage, and it still had its in-service paint and markings. Conveniently, each of the side storage bins is sequentially numbered and labeled, usually with its contents. Translated from Hebrew, the label says 'Storage Bin No.1' with no specific contents. Note also, the welded vehicle identification plate. This feature was added to all armored vehicles following the *Yom Kippur* War, due to an inability to properly identify knocked-out or damaged vehicles where fire had destroyed the painted version.

Yad La'Shiryon, 1992: 'Storage Bin No.2 and No.3' contain more of the same unspecified items. Note that there is a provision for a clip or a lock to further secure the contents, and that there is a virtual history of the vehicle, in the layers of paint. There are at least three distinct shades of sand gray evident here.

Yad La'Shiryon, 1992: This full-length view of the left side shows that all seven bins carry the same sequentially numbered identification for the bins themselves, but there is still no indication of what items may be in them. A significant change in storage ability came,when the height of this part of the hull was increased, since now there was a provision for doors on the previously open-topped bins. Note the drain holes along the bottom of the sponson. The numbers five, six and seven bins also now have lids that open from the top. Below the spare wheel is the exhaust pipe for the auxiliary gasoline motor used to charge the electrical system when the main engine was shut down.

Normally, what appears to be an open access to filler caps is hinged to allow it to be closed. The regular-type filler cap, top right, has the Hebrew letter, '*shin*' for oil. These markings are made from welding wire.

Yad La'Shiryon, 1992: The contents of bins 8 to 13 differ as follows: 'Bin No.8 For Oils', 'Bin No.9 For Oils', 'Bin No.10 5.56 Rounds Regular', 'Bin No.11 Fuse 577 Fuse 557', 'Bin No.12 Fuse 728 Initiator M82', 'Bin No.13 Communications'. Therefore, the lack of specific contents on the left-side labels could mean that they were for miscellaneous crew items. The standard set of tools is carried on this side, while the gun cleaning rods are stowed on the left side.

Yad La'Shiryon, 2005: The once present crew's servicing platform, which also carried the track tensioning spanner on the underside, has been removed. Note the large 'V'-bracket at the rear of the gun breech. When loading, the shell was carried in a rack which was then placed on this to stabilize it during ramming. The bag charges were then loaded behind it. The firing lanyard was inserted through the hole in the center of the breech.

Yad La'Shiryon, 2005: Data stamped into the breech below this hole, indicates that this particular howitzer, an OB (**Ob***usier*) 155-50, was the 193rd produced in 1954, while some other component was the 52nd item produced. Of course, this data is for the weapon alone, not the vehicle.

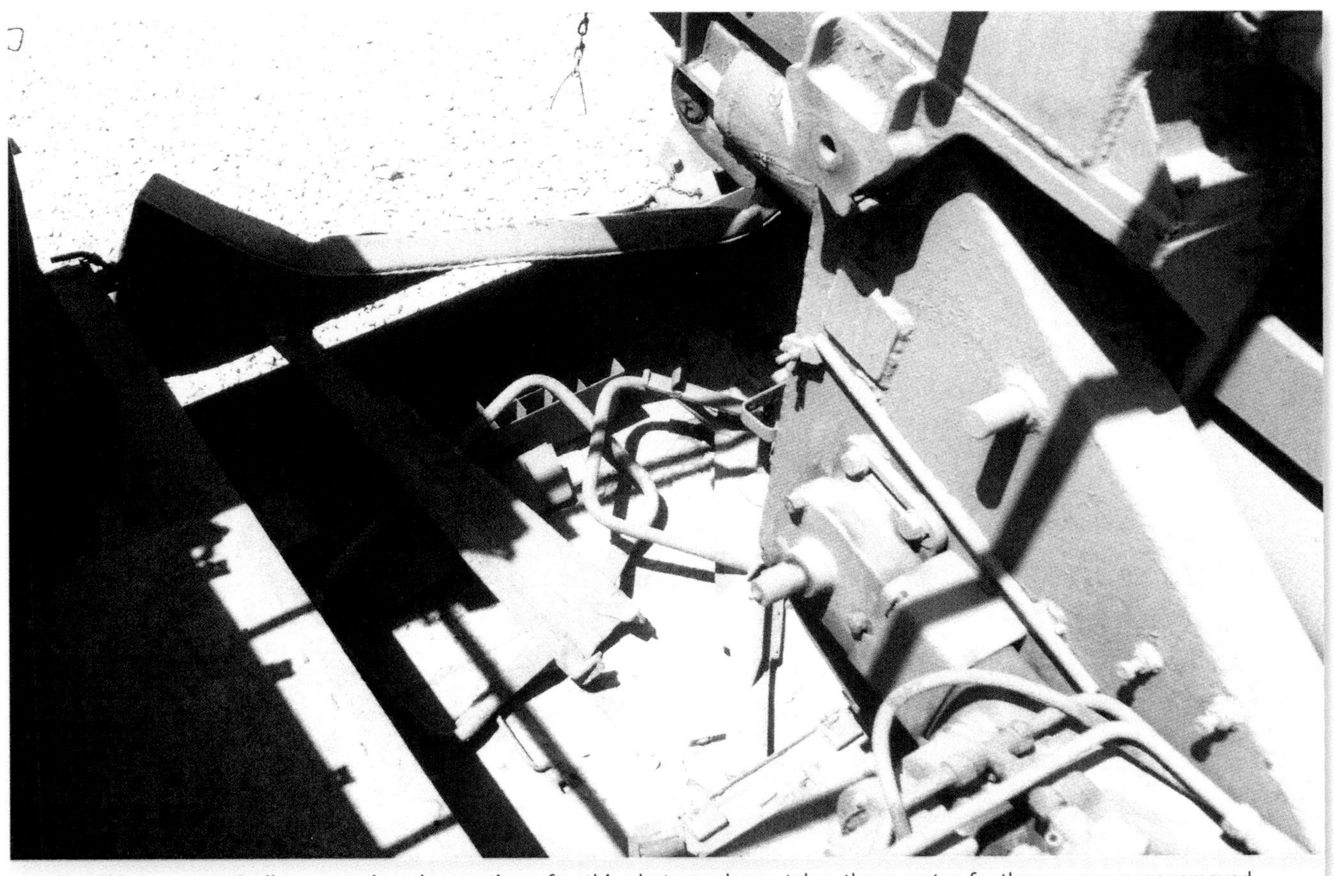

Yad La'Shiryon, 1998: Sadly, as mentioned, sometime after this photograph was taken the rear step for the gun crew was removed. Equally sad, the items on the floor seen here, are also now gone. There are two cradles used to align the projectile with the breech prior to ramming. (Mark Hazzard)

Beit Ha'Totchan, 2008: The large rectangular openings beneath the hull are the cooling air vents originally installed on the Continental version. They were retained, possibly for structural purposes, even though they were no longer needed for ventilation. (Mark Hazzard)

1998: There are some different fittings on this *TOMAT* M50, abandoned on a gun range. Note the large compressed-air tank at the top which was connected to a rammer stowed on the left interior sponson floor. There is no indication on the Latrun display that this feature was ever fitted, either on the exterior or interior. (Mark Hazzard)

1998: The right side is essentially the same as the other vehicles. Note that the idler mount is vertical, indicating it was built on a straight M4A4, not one of the 'stretched' short-hull variants, plus the lack of welds forward of the rear bogie truck. The red tactical sign on the door is repeated on the FDA. The bin labels read: 'Bin No.10 5.56 Rounds Regular', 'Bin No.11 Fuse 577 Fuse 557', 'Bin No.12 Fuse 728 Initiator M82', 'Bin No.13 Communications'. (Mark Hazzard)

This front view shows the massive radiator ventilation louvres to good effect. Also, the red symbol very likely indicates the 5th vehicle in the battalion which normally includes 12 howitzers. The FDA also includes two brackets, held over from the vehicles days as a gun tank. The left one would have helped to secure a coil of barbed wire, while the other was (is) used to hold a tow cable. The two red handles just above the FDA are for the internal engine bay fire extinguisher system. Red is commonly used on IDF vehicles to indicate handles, special fittings and lubrication points. Just visible under the tarp is the driver's alignment vane, used for initial positioning of the vehicle during a firing mission. Note that the registration number, 810172, is only two sequence numbers removed from the Latrun vehicle, 810174. (Mark Hazzard)

This view completes the sequence of bin labels on this side: 'Bin No.8 For Oils', 'Bin No.9 For Oils'. The standard set of tools was carried on this side, while the gun cleaning rods were stowed on the left side. (Mark Hazzard)

This view of the same vehicle confirms that it was common practice to label the left-side bins without any specific contents, just like the *TOMAT* M50 at Latrun back in 1992. (Mark Hazzard)

This view of Bin No.5 is good for more than just the label. It clearly shows the welds from the conversions. Looking into the open bin to the left, one can see the weld from when the profile was raised for the Cummins upgrade. To the right, the top portion of that weld is wider to account for the old exhaust port on the Continental version. (Mark Hazzard)

2008: As for the air tank, this view of the vehicle at *Batey Haosef* shows the compressed air rammer eliminating the need for the multi-person manual version. It is difficult to imagine that this replaced the long pole and the strength of several men, but it is true. The air was fed to the rammer through conduits that pass over the top of the storage locker, then down the inside. This howitzer tube is stuck in the full recoil position. (Jan-Willem de Boer)

1998: This vehicle on the same range is interesting in that it has the serial number 109222, which indicates that it was converted from a captured Egyptian Sherman. Many were captured in 1956, with a few more also in 1967. Egypt used other Sherman versions other than the more well-known M4A4/A2 including the M4A2, M31B1 TRV, M32B1 ARV, based on the cast hull M4A1, and possibly the M4. The last two would be retrofitted with the twin GM diesel engine pack from the M4A2. This vehicle lacks the tactical markings and red paint seen in the previous photographs. (Mark Hazzard)

2008: Based on the welded number plate, this is the same vehicle ten years later with a little more wear, and it may be in a different location on the range. It looks as though the engine is missing, and there is some slight damage from near hits. The barrel is beyond full recoil due to empty cylinders and long-term neglect. Also, the compressed-air tank is now missing. (Mark Hazzard)

2008: Once again, peeling layers of paint reveal at least three different shades of sand gray, lighter to darker. At one time, as seen on in-service vehicles, the rear doors were painted white to assist with station-keeping on the move and to locate vehicles surrounded by the smoke of battle. When zooming in on the original digital image, there is no evidence of a welded insert, confirming that this vehicle is converted from an M4A4. (Mark Hazzard)

1998: Tubes containing powder bags were stored in the large rear bins. Visible running down the right side of this bin is the gas line for the compressed air-assisted rammer. This is a later feature added after the *Yom Kippur* War, as none are visible in period photographs. It is also a feature of the M71 towed 155mm howitzer manufactured by Soltam. The M71 was developed from the Soltam M68, itself a derivative of the M50 howitzer mounted in this vehicle. (Mark Hazzard)

1998: Each side held 16 tubes. The tubes rest on a skeleton of metal bars, as shown here. The small open-top box at the base is for storing aiming stakes. Published color photographs show red/blue and red/white poles on different vehicles. (Mark Hazzard)

Beit Ha'Totchan, 2009: The powder bag and its storage tube are typical of those carried by, and used on, the *TOMAT* M50. (Itamar Rotlevi)

These five 155mm shells are displayed in front of the *TOMAT* M50 at *Beit Ha'Totchan*.

The stenciling on this shell, displayed inside the main building at *Beit Ha'Totchan*, says 'M107' which may be confusing given the IDF's use of the American 175mm Gun M107. However, similar stenciling can be seen on M50 155mm projectiles in a photograph shown earlier in service. (Itamar Rotlevi)

The next eight photographs were taken in a storage yard. Four of them are of the same vehicle from different angles, and all offer further insight into some of the features already described. For instance, the fourth bin has clips set at an angle, purpose unknown. Weld seams in the other three behind it give an idea of the way the conversion was done. The weld seam in the forward bin shows just how much higher the Cummins engine deck is, compared to the earlier Continental deck. (Michael Mass)

As with other vehicles with peeling paint, there are several shades of sand gray. The oldest color is quite light, compared to the top layer. Note that the ID number, 811-159, is a different style than what was commonly seen. It is also different from this same registration as it was seen in two earlier photos. In the first instance, it was prior to the Six-Day War, during the 1966 Independence Day parade, in Haifa. At that time, it was still powered by the Continental and it was fitted with VVSS. The later photo was taken during a *Yom Kippur* War victory parade, after it was upgraded to become a *TOMAT* M50 155mm *MAZKOM Rachav*. (Michael Mass)

There are some interesting features in this view. For one, the registration number is not hyphenated on the rear. This is also a good close-up look at the raised rear platform, plus the two jerrican racks, with fire extinguisher brackets on them. While it is presently unknown what the '5 *alef*' on the left means, the welded numbers are a post-1973 answer on how to identify burned-out vehicles. Note the lack of a number in the battalion marking. To the right are several *Sho't* tanks. (Michael Mass)

In this view of the left side of 811-159, the secondary air tank is missing giving a better view of the various brackets and lines leading to the rammer, on the other side. Note also the markings on this tank. The large rectangular brackets are for the aiming stakes, while the smaller ones above, are for the gun cleaning rod and barrel swab. (Michael Mass)

By zooming in on the original digital image, it is possible to see a manufacturing date of 1955 stamped into the breech. The original 120 howitzers were purchased from surplus NATO stocks, so the actual build dates vary, as can be seen in the photos in this book. The red Hebrew lettering to the left says 'nitrogen', as a coolant, for the breech, with the number '120' indicating, perhaps, the PSI (**P**ounds per **S**quare **I**nch). (Michael Mass)

This vehicle, 810-160, is also shown on the Golan Heights during the *Yom Kippur* War. Note the black paint on the clamp for barbed wired stowage which was standard for identifying items that required regular maintenance. Red paint was also used for the same purpose. The two handles in the small housing are the external triggers for the fire suppression system for the engine compartment. (Michael Mass)

The marking on the rear of this vehicle, and on its FDA in the previous photo, identifies it as the 4th *TOMAT* M50, in the same battalion. As with some other vehicles shown here, this tube is resting in full recoil. Older weapons and vehicles like this will not be regularly maintained. (Michael Mass)

Also belonging to the 4th battery, as indicated by the faint '4' on a faded red background, the number 109176 means that the original tank from which it was converted was a Sherman captured from Egypt, probably in 1956. (Michael Mass)

Beit Ha'Totchan, 2005: This view gives a close-up look at several features, such as the driver's sight vane and details of the gun travel lock. As mentioned previously, the driver's sight was used to align the vehicle, with the first aiming stake. Note the weld seam, just above the jerrican holder. This again shows the additional height of the Cummins engine deck over the original Continental version. The driver's hatch area is also different from the earlier hull. There is a cooling air vent on the right, for the auxiliary gasoline engine.

Beit Ha'Totchan, 2005: This view shows the aforementioned rammer, albeit on the floor of the compartment instead of in its normal stowage bracket on the sponson, as well as the ammunition storage below the howitzer mount. There is storage for 15 shells in locked tubes here, plus 12 more along the sides, for a total of 27 shells on-board. Note the idler mounts and the two rifle racks above the bracket for the rammer, on the left. (Joshua Weingarten)

Beit Ha'Totchan, 2005: Here are two views of the sight vane, front and back. From both angles, one can see the two parts which must be aligned precisely with the aiming stake, downrange. This is also a detail view of the rear of the travel lock. (Joshua Weingarten)

Beit Ha'Totchan, 2005: The data stamping on the breech identifies this as number '714', originally produced in 1953, with later dates of 1955 and 1956, possibly for service.

Beit Ha'Totchan, 2008: This close-up view shows the inside part of the idler mount. From this perspective, there is nothing to identify this vehicle's lineage as a Sherman. The '129' from the engine deck, shown earlier, is repeated here. (Mark Hazzard)

Beit Ha'Totchan, 2005: On the forward bulkhead are the racks for the field telephone/radio and the folding table or shelf. Six ready-round racks line each side. For easy removal, the bases were hinged to fall forward as the round was released. There is also a folding crewman seat.

Yad La'Shiryon, 2005: This is an overhead view of the command area. The socket to the right is for the radio antenna. Note the storage for charts, maps or other paperwork in the folding shelf. Compare this view to the one shown earlier.

Beit Ha'Totchan, 2005: This is a view along the left side, showing the ready round storage and the two previously mentioned rifle racks. Note the thin air line which runs from the rammer over the top of the ammunition bin, to the air tanks on the other side. The larger cables are part of the field telephone and radio system. Although unseen because of the vegetation, the telephone cable reel is folded over the side.

Compare the previous photograph with this one of the *Yad La'Shiryon* display. As viewed from several different angles, there is no apparent provision for the compressed-air rammer. The cables shown here are part of the communication system, some of which, specifically the telephone cable reel, is missing. However, the hinge for it is on the side.

The *Batey Haosef* display, however, has not only the air line, seen here between the rifle clips, but it has two cable reels. (Mark Hazzard)

Yad La'Shiryon, 1992: The right side is not quite as cluttered. There is a crew seat and the six ready-rounds, but not much else.

Yad La'Shiryon, 1992: The front of the right-side powder storage bin is rather plain. Usually, camouflage netting and weather tarps were carried in the internal and external racks.

Yad La'Shiryon, 1992: This is the base of the howitzer mount. Note the lift ring with a duplicate on the other side which appear to be, but are not, part of the gun mount. The following 10 photos provide an all-around look at the howitzer below the side armor, as well as a general view of the interior details.

Batey Haosef, 2008: This angle allows a view of the large size, and number, of the bolts used,to secure the rear of the mount to the vehicle using a 90-degree metal plate. The standard mount was lifted from the field carriage with only a few noticeable changes. The cabling is more complex than on the field mount. Note the rifle rack on the right. (Mark Hazzard)

This is a rear-view of the elevation mechanism, including the twin belts and the toothed gear, as seen from beneath. (Joshua Weingarten)

Yad La'Shiryon, 2005: This view shows the right-side cabling in more detail. Note the lift rings welded to the floor, as well as the large bolts securing the forward portion of the gun mount.

Yad La'Shiryon, 2005: This shows the same area from the rear. The stamping on the side of the mount is in Hebrew which was added, obviously, after the gun's acquisition.

The *Beit Ha'Totchan* mount has a step plate attached, the bolts for which are also evident on the Latrun display.

Note the red lettering on the underside of this vehicle from a storage yard. It matches the lettering, not shown, seen on the *Yad La'Shiryon* display, in 1992, so it is likely common to most, if not all, of the *TOMAT* M50s. As a reminder to the crew, it reads, "lower barrel before moving". (Michael Mass)

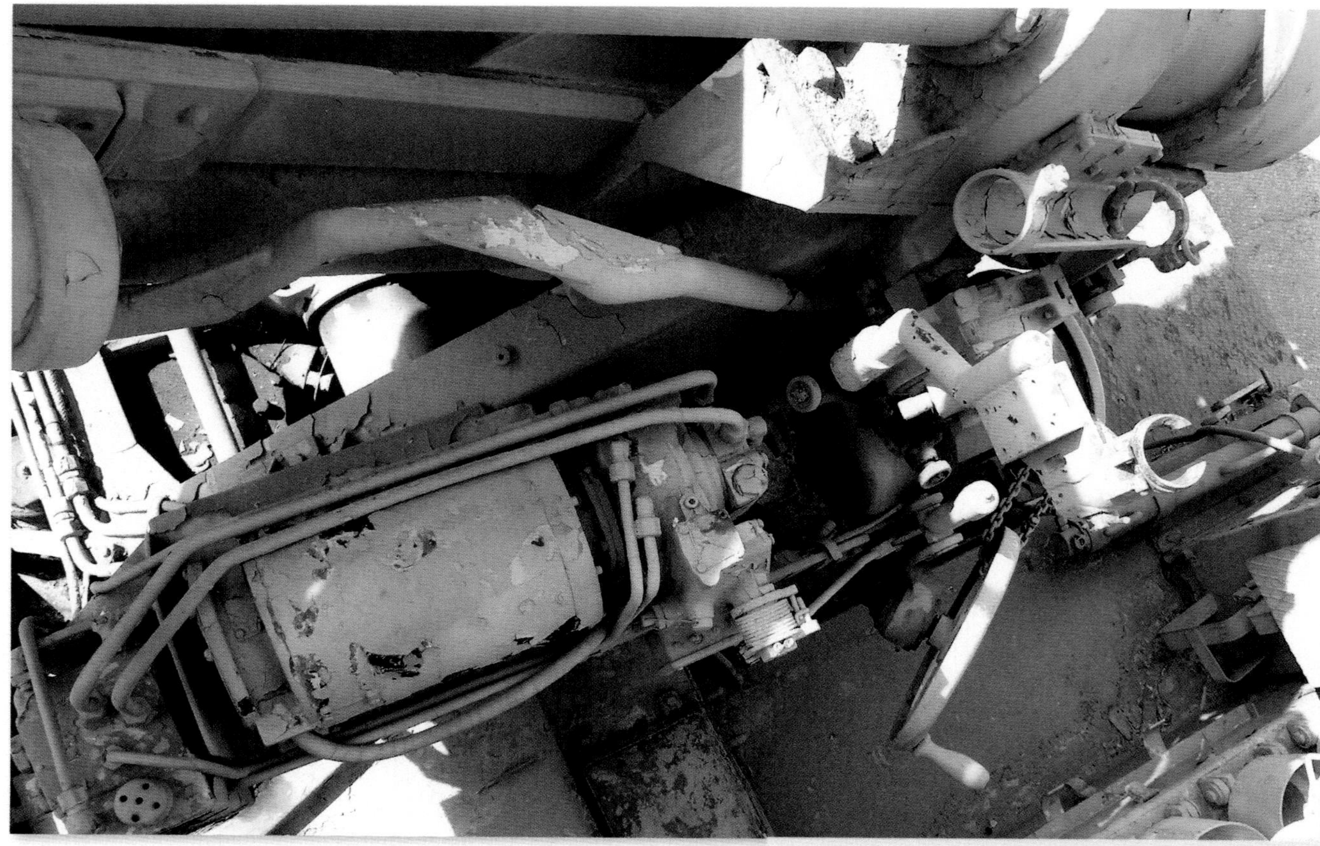

Batey Haosef: An overhead view of the left side, with the gun sight missing. (Mark Hazzard)

Batey Haosef: This photo shows the rear of the same area as that shown above. (Mark Hazzard)

Beit Ha'Totchan, 2005: The bracket, on top of the howitzer tube is a later addition for mounting a live-fire training simulator, not seen on vehicles in action in 1973. The end cap is missing, and the bracket is also missing from the field version in earlier service photographs. It is, however, mounted on the versions on display in the various museums, as well as on the L33 *Ro'em* (see Volume 2) and the M71.

Beit Ha'Totchan, 2005: These views of the howitzer show a more complete gun sight mount, including from the front. The second photo also shows the hinges on the front, used to fold the command shelf and, more importantly, the brackets used to secure it while the vehicle is in motion in a non-combat scenario. The earlier views show the holes in the frame through which the bolts go.

Batey Haosef, 2005: This howitzer is also stuck in recoil due to empty cylinders. One of the fascinating aspects of studying IDF vehicles, of almost any kind, is that one never knows what to really expect, since there is so much variety, especially among vehicles that underwent conversions and upgrades in batches, over time, as with the *TOMAT* M50 155mm SP howitzer series. There is an unusual bracket on the front of this one, perhaps a folding platform for a crewman cleaning the gun tube.

Batey Haosef, 2005: As with the Latrun vehicle, this one was converted using a standard M4A4 hull. Unlike the vehicle at *Yad'Lashiryon*, this one has the two tanks for the air rammer.

Batey Haosef, 1998: This unobstructed view of the deck, with the various hatches closed, will put the following set of photographs into perspective.

Beit Ha'Totchan, 2005: Looking straight down into the driver's compartment, the transmission is to the left in the photograph. The driver's instrument panel is under the deck, to the right. The engine compartment firewall is to the top of the photograph. (Joshua Weingarten)

Beit Ha'Totchan, 2005: This is the fuel tank for the gasoline-driven auxiliary motor. The motor itself is just to the left of the driver, and the exhaust pipe is directly beneath the spare wheel, just visible beneath the open hatch lid.

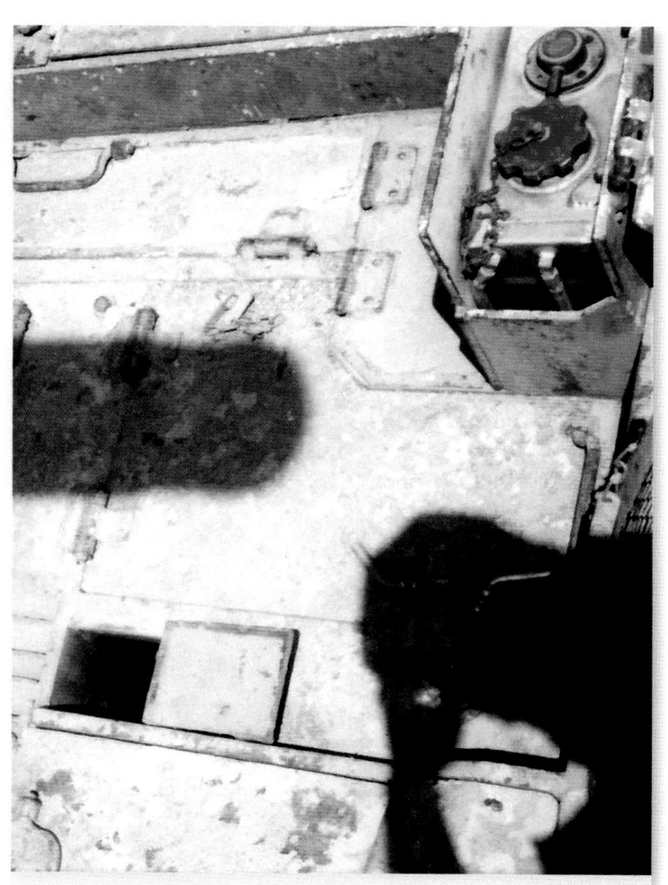

Shown closed in the photo below, this filler cap is in a location appropriate for the transmission fluid, but this is not confirmed. Unfortunately, the typical Hebrew letter for such a thing is not available here.

Batey Haosef, 2008: The Cummins engine is reversed from its position in the normal gun tank. The final drives and transmission are also in the front, even though the driveshaft extends backward from the engine, as seen deep into the opening. It then reverses itself through differential joints to go alongside the engine, forward to the transmission. (Mark Hazzard)

Batey Haosef, 2008: The right-hand radiator fan housing is visible through the open hatch. Note the exhaust in the cutout, to the right. (Mark Hazzard)

Batey Haosef, 2008: The exhaust pipe is visible to the left. It exits from the top of the engine and then out to the vehicle's right. The yellow pipe is for the radiator coolant. (Mark Hazzard)

Batey Haosef, 2008: The driveshaft actually extends beneath the gun mount, before returning alongside the engine. The rectangular object above the shaft is a standard Sherman engine oil cleaner, usually seen mounted vertically on the firewall inside the fighting compartment of gun tanks. (Mark Hazzard)

Batey Haosef, 2008: In a standard Cummins gun-tank installation, the yellow air cleaner is inside the forward part of the hull, and the smaller portion, to its left in the photo, is in the engine bay. This is the cylindrical object visible through the small access hatches in a standard Cummins deck. (Mark Hazzard)

Batey Haosef, 2008: This is the left side cleaner. The photograph also gives a clearer view of the oil cleaner. Note the fuel line exiting one of the fuel tanks. (Mark Hazzard)

Photos of actual *MAPIK* half-tracks are difficult to find. There are many shots of command and communications vehicles, but fire-control versions have certain features, the most important of which is difficult to see. That feature is the table used for the calculations. At the time that the half-track was in use in this capacity, all such calculations were done by hand. This *MAPIK* from 1967 does, indeed have the table, at the right rear. (Defense Establishment Archives)

In this photo, also from the Six-Day War, the table is more readily discernable. It is also to the rear of the vehicle, since it gave the fire-control team more space. The radios and field telephone equipment were at the front, so movement there could be somewhat restricted. (Defense Establishment Archives)

The War of Attrition was truly an artilleryman's conflict. For its duration, self-propelled artillery units were regularly rotated in and out of the combat area, so mobility was key. I have a friend, an IDF Artillery Corps veteran who wishes to remain anonymous, who functioned as part of the fire-control team in 402 Battalion, equipped with the *TOMAT* M50 155mm SP howitzer. This photo shows a portion of 402 Battalion as it crosses the Sinai Desert, most likely heading toward the Suez Canal, or along its length. The third vehicle in line is a battery *MAPIK* half-track. (Photographed by a member of the 402 Battalion)

This is my friend's *MAPIK* in its position behind the Suez Canal. Normally, for both weather-protection purposes and clear vision for the calculations, the team operated with the vehicle's weather tarp in place. Note that this vehicle also has a table, typically used for maps, over the windscreen, as did most others. To the right, and in the background, is one of the howitzers in its dug-in position. (Photographed by a member of 402 Battalion)

This wider view, in a different location, shows the battery's vehicles moving into their dispersed positions. The same MAPIK is at the left-center of the picture, with another very common support vehicle, an M601 Dodge Power Wagon.

Here is a clear look at the rear of a *MAPIK*, also during the War of Attrition in 1969. The team member is on the field telephone, probably relaying firing instructions to the battery commander. His hand is covering his ear, likely to obstruct some of the noise of combat. This position is more or less permanent, given the deployed sunscreen and the liquid refreshment on top of the stowage rack. Note the forward tarp, on the right, which reads 'US Mail'. (Defense Establishment Archives)

This *MAPIK* is in a similar dug-in position but, this time, it is during the *Yom Kippur* War in 1973. It is quite possible that the actual location is along Artillery Road, a little back from the Bar-Lev Line, along which the mobile units travelled as they changed positions during the War of Attrition. There are several points of interest including the spare track carried on the left fender, the white air-recognition stripe, and the fact that the antenna rods poke through holes in the weather tarp. Also, as before, one of the dug-in M50s is in the background. (Defense Establishment Archives)

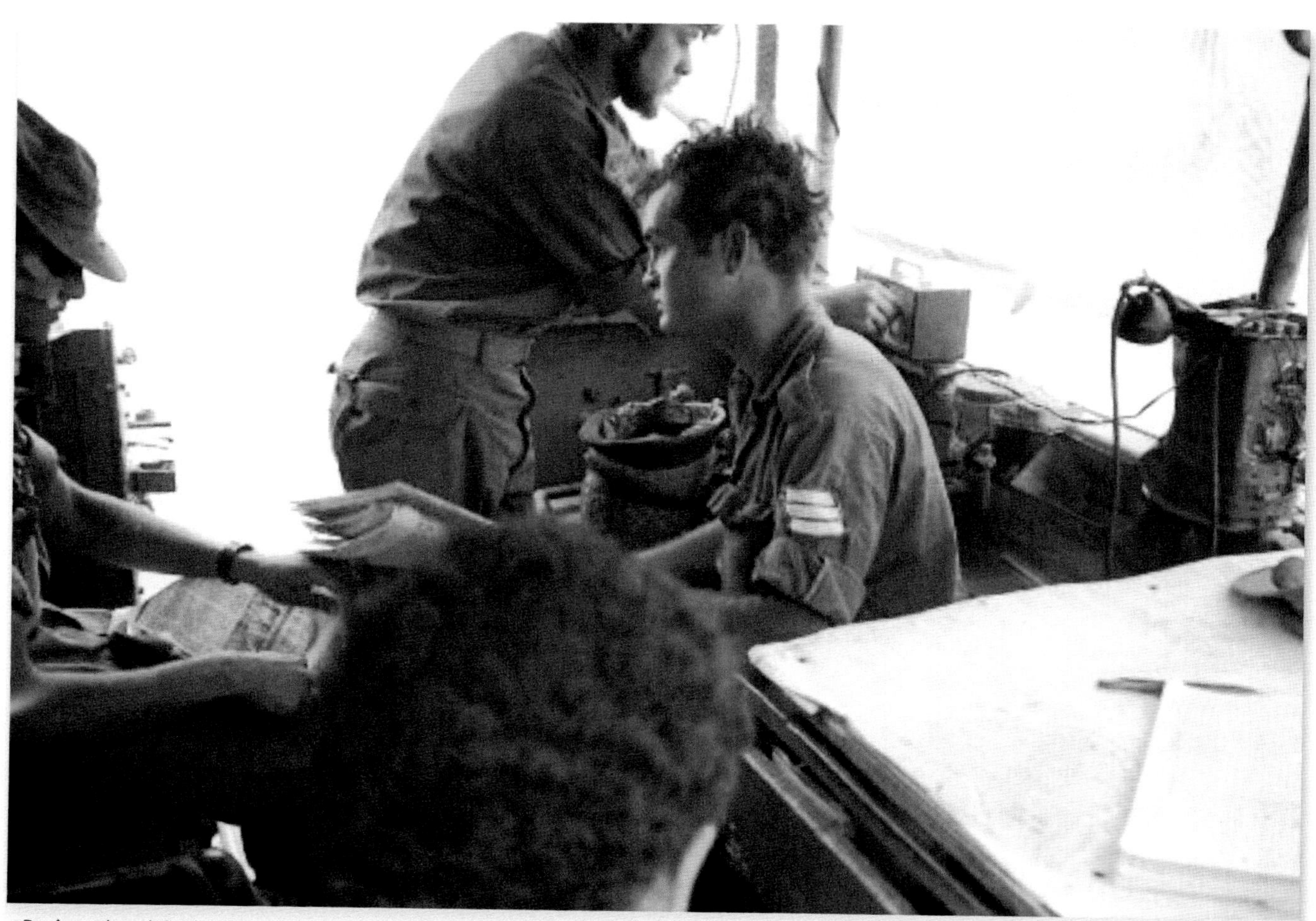

During a break in the action, two fire-control team members read the paper, while the other adjusts the radio, perhaps to a local rock-n-roll station. This photo also offers a good view of the aforementioned table which, in this case, is a little farther forward. Note the bandage on the face of the guy on the right. The second photo is a close-up showing one of the calculations, in progress. (Defense Establishment Archives)

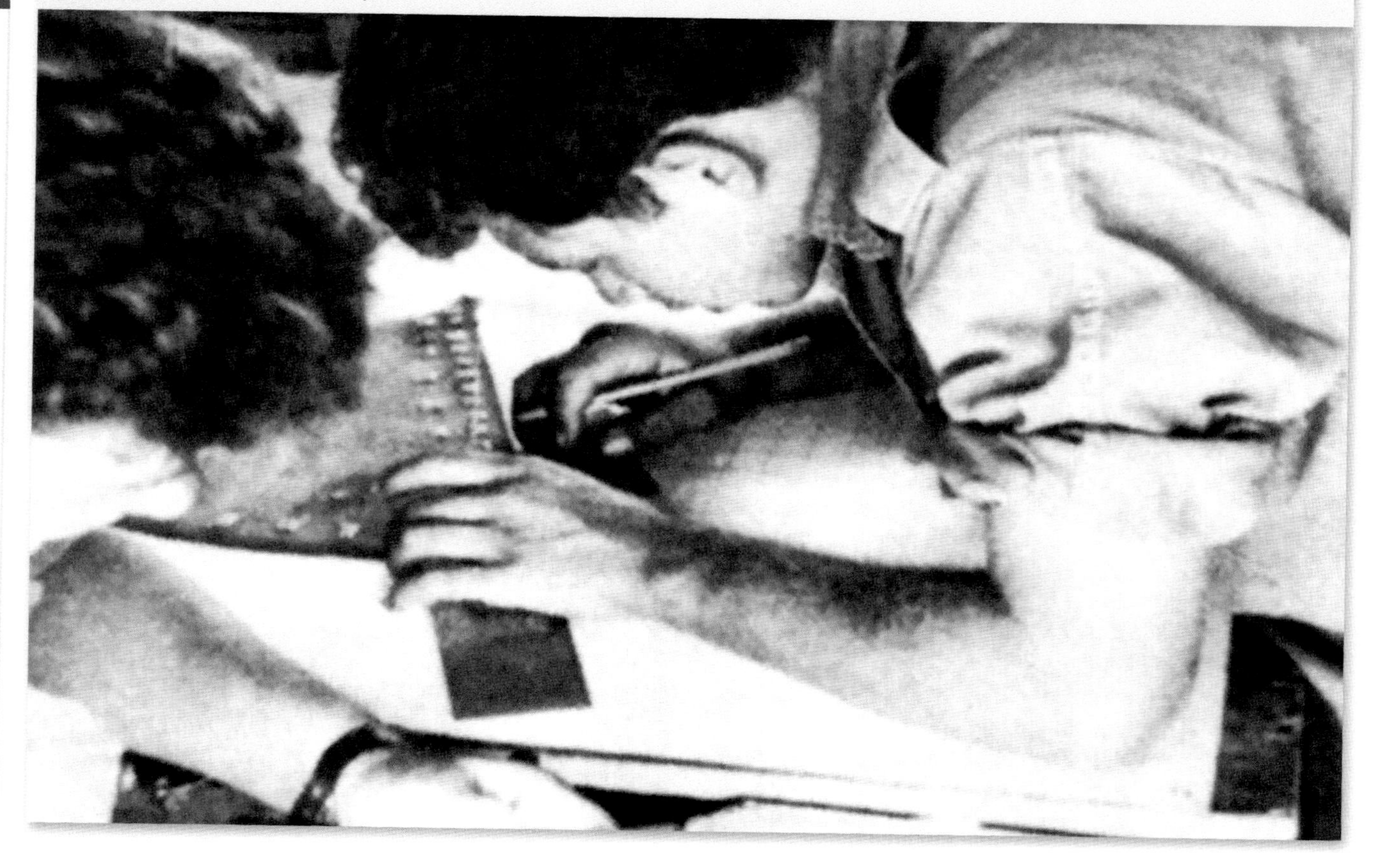

I was unable to see a true and complete *MAPIK* on display in Israel. However, there is this command and communication vehicle at *Yad La'Shiryon* in Latrun, which comes close. It is interesting in several ways, one of which is the fact that it was, at one time, either an M5A1 or an M9A1, rather than an M5, as it may appear at first glance. How do I know that? A careful look at the top of the armored windscreen provides the answer. The right two-thirds of the top section, on the left in the picture, is a strip that was added after the machine gun pulpit was removed. The strip added looks very different from the normal top strip on a straight M5 (the M9 never entered production). Another later feature of IDF half-tracks was the unusual hinge arrangement on the hood. Normally, the sides would fold only toward the center-line, but the hinges here allow the entire hood to be lifted up and back for easier access. Note the rather bent frame for the forward map table.

These interior views show some features that would have been present in a *MAPIK*. First, the framing for the table in the rear is similar to what would be needed for the *MAPIK*'s, but it is much smaller. The seat is similar as well. There is a radio to the front, but there is no apparent provision for a field telephone with its associated cable reel. The spring-loaded platform is for a seat, usually used by the person using the forward map table, while the large tube alongside it would be for a machine gun pedestal, also not normally seen on a *MAPIK*.

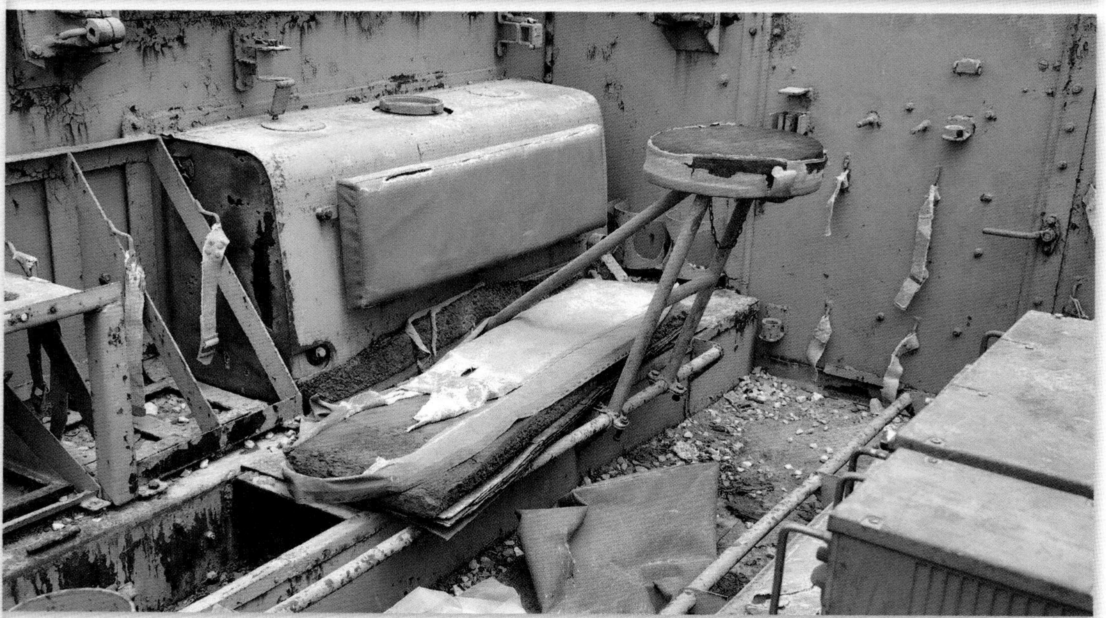

The half-track *MAPIK* was ultimately replaced by the more modern M577, the command version of the M113 series. In general service, it was referred to as a *Mugaf*. However, in the Artillery Corps, it is still a *MAPIK*. Externally, it has been modified from the basic M577 by removing the framed wooden panel from the front and adding the standard IDF side stowage racks and 'towel' bar.

The *Mugaf*-based *MAPIK* is fitted with external diesel generator, mounted in the basket at the front. It provided 24-volt power for all electronic systems and communication equipment when the main engine was shut down. A single generator provided enough power for two vehicles and, if required, the generator could be removed from the vehicle and used as a stationary unit on the ground. (Eran Kaufman)

This nice full-profile view of the right side of the vehicle, plus the right-rear ¾ view, show a few unique IDF features, such as the side rack and stowage box. It also shows the modified exhaust. The IDF extended it, turned it downward and covered it with a metal burn shield. Note the details on the boxes. (Jan-Willem de Boer)

These views of the interior of the M577 version of the *MAPIK* looks a little more complex than its half-track cousin, with plenty of space for electronic equipment. The power produced by the front-mounted generator entered through the junction box below, and to the right, of the commander's hatch. The large number of lights and shelving for radios, etc. certainly justified the need for it. The large door at the bottom right was the internal access to the vehicle's engine, also a diesel. (Jan-Willem de Boer)

There is a *Mugaf (MAPIK?)* with a cutaway view at *Batey Haosef* in Tel Aviv-Yafo, with some equipment and figures. This gives a rough idea of what the relatively confined space may look like inside an active modern *MAPIK*.

The driver's area is pretty much that of a standard *Zelda* (IDF name for the M113, as shown in the first photo. The second photo shows the left-rear of the interior, to generally complete the tour. (Jan-Willem de Boer)

Term	Definition
...im	plural in Hebrew
Alef	Hebrew letter A
Batey Haosef	IDF Collection Houses, in Tel Aviv-Yafo (Jaffa)
Beit Ha'Totchan	Hewbrew for 'Gunners' House' or 'House of Artillerymen', in Zichron Ya'Akov
Bet	Hebrew letter B
Dalet	Hebrew letter D
Degem	Type
EGGED	Collection of artillery battalions, equivalent to a brigade
Egged	Israel Transport Cooperative Society, Ltd = Israel's largest bus company
Episcopi	Hebrew name for Sherman-based rocket launcher
Gimel	Hebrew letter C
Haviv	290mm rockets, mounted on the *Episcopi*
Heil Ha'Shiryon	IDF Armoured Corps
Heil Ha'Totchanim	IDF Artillery Corps
HVSS	Horizontal Volute Spring Suspension (wide tracks)
Ivry	280mm rockets mounted on prototype for *Episcopi*
kibbutz	agricultural settlement
Kilshon	Hebrew name for Sherman-based anti-radar rocket launcher
L33	length of howitzer barrel in *Ro'em*, often used in place of the name
La'Shiryon	Armored Corps Memorial and Museum, in Latrun
ma'oz	'castle keep', used to describe forts along the Bar-Lev Line
MACHMAT	Hebrew acronym for self-propelled heavy mortar
MAZKOM Rachav	Acronym for suspension and tracks, wide
MAZKOM Tzar	Acronym for suspension and tracks, narrow
moshav	collective agricultural settlement
Ro'em	'Thunderous', 155mm self-propelled howitzer on Sherman hull
sandalim	'Sandals', Hebrew slang for recoil wedges
Sayeret Netz	'Reconnaissance Hawk'
ta'oz	'strongholds', behind the Bar-Lev Line, along the 'Artillery Road'
TOMAT	Hebrew acronym for self-propelled gun
TZAHAL	Acronym for Tzva Hagana Le Yisrael = Israel Defence Force (IDF)
Tzidud Rachav	'Turning large' or wide turn, for re-positioning multiple vehicles
VVSS	Vertical Volute Spring Suspension (narrow tracks)
Yishuv	Literally 'settlement', refers to the area occupied by Jews, prior to modern Israel

Sherman Designations		
American	British	Description
M4	Sherman I	75mm, VVSS, dry ammo stowage, 56-degree hull front, small hatch (IC= Firefly)
M4 Composite	Sherman I Hybrid	75mm, VVSS, dry ammo stowage, cast hull front, large hatch (initial small) (IC Hybrid= Firefly)
M4(105)	Sherman IB	105mm, VVSS, 47-degree hull front, large hatch
M4(105)HVSS	Sherman IBY	105mm, HVSS, 47-degree hull front, large hatch
M4A1	Sherman II	75mm, VVSS, dry ammo stowage, small hatch, later w/ large hatch, still dry ammo stowage
M4A1(76)	Sherman IIA	76mm, VVSS, wet ammo stowage, large hatch
M4A1(76)HVSS	Sherman IIAY	76mm, HVSS wet ammo stowage, large hatch
M4A2	Sherman III	75mm, VVSS, dry ammo stowage, later w/ 47-degree hull front, dry ammo stowage
M4A2(76)	Sherman IIIAY	76mm, HVSS, wet ammo stowage, 47-degree hull front
M4A3	Sherman IV	75mm, VVSS, small hatch, dry ammo stowage (M4A3 not used by British)
M4A3(76)	76mm, VVSS, wet ammo stowage, 47-degree hull front, large hatch	
M4A3(76)HVSS	76mm, HVSS, wet ammo stowage, 47-degree hull front, large hatch	
M4A3(105)	105mm, VVSS, 47-degree hull front, large hatch	
M4A3(105)HVSS	Same as above, except suspension	
M4A3E2	'Jumbo', assault tank w/ extra armour, wet ammo stowage, 75mm, w/some upgraded to 76mm	
M4A4	Sherman V	75mm, VVSS, dry ammo stowage, longer hull, 56-degree hull front, small hatch (VC = Firefly)
M4A6	75mm, VVSS, dry ammo stowage, cast hull front (M4A6 not used by British)	
Israeli		
M-3	Sherman with a 75mm Gun M3	
M-1	Sherman with a 76mm Gun M1, M1A1 or M1A2	
Super Sherman	M-1 Sherman with the HVSS suspension	
M-50	French 75mm gun CN-75-50 in round turret, all hull types, except M4A6	
M-51	French 105mm gun D1504 L44 in T23 style turret, large hatch, M4, M4A3, M4A1	

Memorials

There are memorials all over Israel, to honor individuals, units and specific battles. The first M50 howitzer is in Elyachin, a town south of Hadera, in northern Israel. It is dedicated to Master Sergeant Shaked Ozeri, killed on May 4, 2000. He was the last IDF combat death before the final withdrawal from Lebanon. The howitzer is in pristine condition, as a memorial to a fallen soldier should be. Note the stowed firing pedestal and the mount for the training simulator on top. The second M50 howitzer is displayed in Kiryat Chaim, within the municipal limits of Haifa. (Osnat Rotlevi)

Preserved Items (Volume 1)	
Vehicle	**Location**
M7 Priest	*Beit Ha'Totchan* (Gunner's House or House of Artillerymen) near Zichron Ya'Akov, on the coast between Haifa (22.8 miles north) & Tel Aviv (43 miles south)
Priest Bunker	Kibbutz Kinneret, 6.5 miles south of Tiberias
TOMAT M50	*Beit Ha'Totchan*
TOMAT M50	*Yad La'Shiryon* (IDF Armored Corps Memorial & Museum), approx. 17 mileswest of Jerusalem
TOMAT M50	*Batey Haosef* (IDF Collection Houses), in Tel Aviv-Yafo
M5 Half-track *Zachlam* or *Zachlad* (diesel)	*Yad La'Shiryon* (Command & Communications)
M577 *Mugaf*	*Beit Ha'Totchan* and *Batey Haosef*

Gun/Howitzer	Location
Napoleonchik	*Beit Ha'Totchan*, Yad Mordechai & Tiberias
75mm *Saint Chamond-Mondragon (Cucaracha)*	*Batey Haosef*
Canon de 105 mle 1913 Schneider	*Batey Haosef*
QF (Quick Firing)-3.7-inch Mountain Gun	*Batey Haosef*
Canon de 75mm modele 1897	*Batey Haosef*
Krupp 75mm Model 1903	*Beit Ha'Totchan, Batey Haosef, Beit Ha'Gdudim* Museum (near Netanya) , Rishon Le'Zion
QF (Quick Firing) 25-pounder	*Beit Ha'Totchan, Batey Haosef*
Obusiers de 155mm Mle 1950 (M50) howitzer	*Beit Ha'Totchan, Batey Haosef,* Elyachin & Kiryat Chaim

Further Reading

Available from

Trackpad Publishing

Available from:
www.trackpadpublishing.com
www.facebook.com/trackpadpublishing
trackpadpublish@gmail.com

Published by Trackpad Publishing

18 Sandown Close
Blackwater
Camberley
Surrey
GU17 0EL
UK

www.trackpadpublishing.com
trackpadpublish@gmail.com

History of the IDF Artillery Corps
Israeli Sherman-based Self-Propelled Weapons, Volume 1
Tom Gannon
978-0-9928425-8-1

Designed and produced by Michael Shackleton

Printed by Scandinavian Book, c/o LaserTryk.co.uk Ltd. Hamilton House, Mabledon Place, Bloomsbury, WC1H 9BB

Comments or Corrections

While every effort has been made to ensure that the information contained herein is correct, some factual or typographical errors may be present. Should you detect an error, or simply wish to make a comment regarding this publication, please contact the publisher at any of the links above.